George L. Craik

Outlines of the History of the English Language

For the use of the junior classes in colleges and the classes in schools

George L. Craik

Outlines of the History of the English Language
For the use of the junior classes in colleges and the classes in schools

ISBN/EAN: 9783337084387

Printed in Europe, USA, Canada, Australia, Japan

Cover: Foto ©Paul-Georg Meister /pixelio.de

More available books at **www.hansebooks.com**

Outlines

OF THE

HISTORY OF THE ENGLISH LANGUAGE

FOR

THE USE OF THE JUNIOR CLASSES IN COLLEGES AND
THE HIGHER CLASSES IN SCHOOLS.

BY

GEORGE L. CRAIK,

PROFESSOR OF HISTORY AND OF ENGLISH LITERATURE IN
QUEEN'S COLLEGE, BELFAST.

Sixth Edition, Revised and Improved.

LONDON:
CHAPMAN AND HALL, 193, PICCADILLY.

1867.

ADVERTISEMENT.

THESE OUTLINES are an abstract from a portion of the Course of Lectures delivered in the Class of the English Language in Queen's College, Belfast, which is attended by undergraduates of the first year; but the work has been drawn up with the design of presenting a connected though succinct view of the essentials of its subject, and so as to be adapted for the general reader as well as for being used as a Text-book in any place of education in which English Philology is one of the departments of study.

To the series of propositions printed in a larger type, which embody the leading facts constituting the History of the Language, and which perhaps might be advantageously committed to memory by young persons, have been subjoined the more important of those minor and subsidiary particulars brought forward in the Lectures of which I had been accustomed to direct that notes should be taken.

In this way the student or reader is put in possession of all the information necessary for the complete understanding of the general statements, and for following the survey of the subject so far as they carry it.

Compendious, too, and elementary as the book is, it is constructed in part with a view to its serving as an introduction both to English History and to so much of the great modern science of Ethnology as depends upon the descent and relationship of languages.

In this new Edition the work has again been carefully revised throughout, and, although not much has been altered, a few slight additions have been introduced here and there. The customary terms *Saxon* and *Anglo-Saxon* have now been everywhere discarded, as not only unauthorised by the facts of the case, but self-contradictory and eminently misleading. If the people were *Saxons*, and the language *Saxon*, before the Norman Conquest, nothing in that catastrophe could possibly have converted either the one or the other into *English*. But, in truth, they have been always *English;*—which is, and can be, the only reason why they are *English* now.

January, 1864.

CONTENTS.

ILLUSTRATIVE SPECIMENS.

OUTLINES,

&c.

I. There are two kinds of Evidence by which the origin or composition of any product may be attested:— the Internal; and the External, or Historical.

THE distinction is, that the Internal Evidence is furnished by the product itself; the External, by something else.

And any fact considered in reference to the causes or circumstances out of which it may have arisen, or by which it may have been brought about, is a product.

External Evidence is usually the clearer and more precise in its intimations, as well as the more obtrusive or the more readily come by; it is in these respects like other superficial or outside things; but Internal Evidence, when its interpretation is free from doubt, is the more trustworthy and conclusive. It is the pure reason of the case, speaking to us directly, by which we cannot be deceived if we only rightly apprehend it. The mind, however, is not satisfied without a concurrence of the two kinds of evidence whenever the case seems to admit of it.

It is very rarely, if ever, that Internal Evidence is ab-

B

solutely wanting; External Evidence frequently is. A familiar instance of evidence which is purely internal, and yet sufficient, is that with which Paley sets out in his work on *Natural Theology*, of a watch in motion found by a person who had never seen or heard of such a contrivance, but who at once and without any doubt infers it to be the work of an intelligent and designing mind. His inference to that extent could hardly have been strengthened by the addition of any amount of external evidence.

In other questions, however, such as that of who wrote a book of unknown or disputed authorship, or who painted a particular picture, the internal evidence, which we always have, and without which in such a case no accumulation of external evidence would be enough to produce perfect conviction, at least to a mind of any critical sagacity, is usually endowed with much greater power of securing our acquiescence and reliance when it has the support of external evidence.

It is the same with questions relating to the origin, or affiliation and connexion, of languages. Here, too, the internal evidence, or that presented by the languages themselves, is indispensable, and is the main consideration; but such external evidence as is to be had is not to be disregarded. It demands, at least, always to be explained, and to be shown to be consistent with the internal evidence; and it sometimes serves as a useful index to the direction in which the internal evidence is to be looked for or pursued.

Were it only for the latter reason, it would be convenient in questions of this nature to take the External or Historical evidence as the basis of our inquiries; but it is also natural to begin with that, as consisting usually of facts that were well known long before much or almost any attention was drawn to the Internal evidence.

II. The First of the facts constituting the External or Historical Evidence that we have in regard to the sources of the English language is, that the country in which it is spoken and has grown up appears clearly to have been once occupied, in whole or in part, by a Celtic population.

I. The earliest express statement that has come down to us in regard to the language spoken in the country now called England is that of Tacitus, who, writing in the first century of our era, says (*Agricola*, 11) of those of the Britons of his day who were nearest to Gaul, that they were probably of Gallic extraction, and that their speech was not very different from that of the Gauls (*sermo haud multum diversus*).

But Cæsar (*B. G.* v. 12), writing a century before Tacitus, although he says nothing about the language of the Britons, in asserting as a fact what Tacitus advances as a probability, that the Britons dwelling along the coast opposite to Gaul had originally come from that country, particularises *Belgium* as the part of Gaul whence they had emigrated; and elsewhere (I. 1, and II. 4) he tells us that the Belgæ were for the greater part of Germanic descent, and that both they and the Aquitani differed in language, as well as in institutions and laws, from the proper Gauls, or Celts as they were called in their own tongue.

It has thence been argued by some speculators that the language of this portion of the population of Britain must, when the country first became known to the Romans, have been not a Celtic but a Germanic language. This view was first proposed by the Scottish antiquary, Sir John Clerk of Pennicuick, in a "Dissertation on the Ancient Language of Britain," written in 1742, but first published in 1782, in the first volume of the *Bibliotheca Topographica Britannica;* and it was afterwards taken up and maintained, with his usual cleverness and plausibility, by John Pinkerton, in his "Enquiry into the History of Scotland preceding the Reign of Malcolm III." (2 vols. 8vo, Edinburgh, 1789; republished in 1794 and in 1814). Pinkerton states (I. 363) that he had not happened to see Clerk's Dissertation till after the materials for his own work were collected.

It is still, however, matter of dispute whether the language of the Belgians was Germanic or Celtic. It is contended by many that Cæsar's statement can only mean that they spoke a different dialect from the people of Celtic Gaul; and that, if they were Germans by descent, they had, after their settlement in Gaul, exchanged their ancestral speech for the common language of that country.

II.   In this undecided state of the question respecting the language of the Belgæ, recourse has been had, for evidence in regard to the earliest language spoken in Britain, to the ancient topographical nomenclature of the country, that is, the oldest names of places and natural objects in it. These, which are always originally significant, are the surest evidence we can have in regard to the language spoken in any country at the time when they were imposed. The ancient topographical nomenclature of Britain is elaborately investigated by George Chalmers in the first volume of his *Caledonia* (3 vols. 4to, 1810—24); and the subject has also been more recently discussed by the late Rev. Richard Garnett in a paper printed in the *Proceedings of the Philological Society* (i. 119). Whatever differences of opinion may still exist upon subordinate points, there is now no dissent from the general conclusion arrived at by both of these writers, that the oldest topographical nomenclature everywhere in Britain is Celtic. This is the case in the parts of the country which Cæsar states to have been colonized from Belgic Gaul, as well as elsewhere. *Kent*, for instance, is a Celtic name, and *Thames* is a Celtic name. Mr Garnett further holds the topographical nomenclature of France and that of ancient South Britain to belong to the same form of the Celtic, namely, the Cambrian, or Welsh; and he conceives that to be the earliest and least corrupted form now subsisting.

It should be observed, however, that the fact of the most ancient topographical nomenclature of the Belgic parts of Gaul and Britain being Celtic does not prove that the Belgic colonists in either case spoke a Celtic language; for the names may have been imposed by preceding occupants of Celtic race. But it proves that the parts occupied by the Belgic colonists must, as well as the rest of the country, have been at one time in the possession of a Celtic population; which is enough for the purpose in hand.

It may also be mentioned that Mr Garnett's supposition, of the most ancient British topographical names being all Welsh, is inconsistent with a theory which was first put forward by the learned Edward Lhuyd, in the Preface to the Welsh part of his *Archæologia Britannica* (folio, Oxford, 1707).* Lhuyd argues, from the names

---

* Of this Preface, which is in Welsh, there is an English translation in the Third Appendix to Archbish)p Nicholson's *Irish Historical Library.*

of rivers and mountains throughout both Wales and the rest of South Britain, that a Celtic people of the Irish or Gaelic branch must have preceded the Welsh in the occupation of the country; and that these *Gwydhelians*, as he calls them, had been forced by the Welsh to retire for the greater part to the North and to Ireland.

III. But we must be held to have sufficient proof of the general statement at the head of the Section in the standing testimony of the great fact, that a considerable Celtic population, retaining its peculiar speech, still subsists in the occupation of a part of South Britain (the district that we now call Wales), its possession of which is historically known to be of very ancient origin, and cannot be probably accounted for otherwise than upon its own tradition, supported by the whole current of its national literature, that it is the remnant of a race which the Romans found spread over a much larger extent of the country, and the portion of which that escaped destruction, or preserved its independence, on the Saxon invasion, was then forced to retire within its present narrow limits.

III. The Second fact is, that from about the middle of the First Century of our era till after the commencement of the Fifth, or for not much short of 400 years, South Britain was a Province of the Roman Empire, and extensively occupied by colonists speaking the Latin tongue.

THE first Roman invasion of Britain under Julius Cæsar took place late in the summer of the year B.C. 55. According to a calculation of Dr Edmund Halley, the eminent astronomer, published in the *Philosophical Transactions*,* the day was the 26th of August. On this occasion, the Roman general remained only till about the 20th of September, nor did he advance into the country; but he returned in the May of the year following, B.C. 54, when he compelled several of the princes and states in the south-eastern part of the island to surrender and give him hostages.† The Britons were left unmolested and

---

* No. 193 (for March—June, 1691); vol. xvii. p. 495.

† It has generally been supposed that Cæsar on both his expeditions to Britain landed on the east coast between Dover and Deal, having sailed from Wissant, about midway between Boulogne and Calais; but Professor Airy, the Astronomer Royal, has lately argued with great ingenuity that the Portus Itius, from which he embarked, was at the mouth of the Somme, much farther to the south, and that he made his descent on the coast of Sussex, at or near the same point, between Pevensey and Hastings, which was selected for his invasion by William the Norman eleven centuries later. Professor Airy's views were first submitted in an anonymous communication to the *Athenæum*, dated 29th March, 1851; and were afterwards more fully expounded in a paper read before the Society of Antiquaries,

unvisited from this time, till, in B.C. 26, on Augustus threatening a new invasion, they sent an embassy to him in Gaul, and consented to acknowledge the Roman dominion by the payment of tribute. The actual subjugation of Britain, however, did not commence till A.D. 43, in the reign of the Emperor Claudius; nor was it completed before A.D. 84, when Julius Agricola, who had been first appointed to the supreme command there in A.D. 78, in the reign of Vespasian, resigned and returned to Rome in that of Domitian, after having in seven campaigns overrun the country to a considerable distance beyond the Forth, and also sailed round the island and reduced the Orkneys.

The Roman dominion ceased to be acknowledged by the Britons in A.D. 409, in the reign of the Emperor Honorius; and in A.D. 418, according to the National Chronicle, "the Romans collected all the treasures that were in Britain, and some they hid in the earth, so that no one has since been able to find them; and some they carried with them into Gaul." The account given by the native historian Ethelwerd (writing in Latin in the tenth century) is, that in this year those of the Roman race who were left in Britain, not being able to endure the multiplied menaces of the natives, buried their treasure in holes dug in the earth (*scrobibus*), imagining that they might have an opportunity of recovering it after-

8th and 22d January, 1852, and printed in the *Archæologia*, vol. xxxiv. pp. 231—250. London, 1852.

But see "The Invasion of Britain by Julius Cæsar;" by Thomas Lewin, Esq., of Trinity College, Oxon. Lon. 1859. Mr Lewin makes out a very plausible case for Cæsar having sailed from Boulogne, and landed at what is now called *Romney Marsh*,—a name which he believes still preserves the memory of the event.

wards, a thing which never happened; and, taking only a part of it with them, assembled at or on the water (*in unda*), set sail, and retired to Gaul. The earlier narrative of Gildas, which is of the sixth century, but is extremely confused and obscure, contains nothing to this effect, but speaks of Ambrosius Aurelianus, whom Beda and other writers place at the head of the Britons in the latter part of the fifth century, as the only individual of Roman extraction who was then left alive in the island.

It is in the highest degree improbable that the retirement or expulsion of the inhabitants of Roman descent can have been so complete as these statements would make it. From the number of settlements which both history and their remains on or under the soil prove the Romans to have possessed in all parts of the country, from the Channel to the Friths of Forth and Clyde, comprehending many towns and villas, as well as mere military stations, it is evident that in the space of between three and four centuries, during which the island had been a Roman province, it had been extensively colonised, like most of the other provinces, from the original central seat of the empire, and that the portion of its population thus formed must in all likelihood have been very considerable and very widely diffused.

But, although it cannot be doubted that an extended Latin civilisation grew up in Britain in the course of the long space of time that it continued under the Roman dominion, we are not informed by any express notices in the ancient writers in how far Latin became the language of the country. Tacitus, however, affirms (*Agric.* 21), that already by A.D. 79, when Agricola had made his second campaign, the sons of the chiefs, under his judicious measures, were beginning to be attracted to liberal studies, and to be becoming ambitious of excelling in the eloquent

use of the Roman tongue, which they had heretofore de-
spised.   And Juvenal about the same early date speaks
(*Sat.* xv. 111) of the art of oratorical pleading being taught
to the Britons by their eloquent neighbours the Gauls,
and of the feeing of counsel being now practised even in
Thule.   Agricola, Tacitus tells us, preferred (or, at least,
professed to prefer) the natural genius of the Britons to
the studied acquirements of the Gauls.*

From the name of the Saxon Border (*Limes Saxonicus*)
having been borne in the Roman time by a portion of the
eastern and south-eastern coast of Britain (from Brano-
dunum, now Brancaster, in Norfolk, to the Portus Adurni,
probably either Pevensey or Aldrington, in Sussex), it
has been argued that the Saxons must have already
established themselves in some portion of this district.
But the only Saxon settlement that could have given rise
to the name would have been a settlement extending over
the whole line of coast so denominated; and it is impossible that that should have passed unrecorded.   There
seems to be no reasonable objection to the commonly
received interpretation of the name, as meaning simply
the coast along which the Saxon pirates were wont to
make their descents.†
    Many small bodies of barbarians, however, were trans-

* See upon this subject a paper by Dr Latham in the transactions
of the Historical Society of Lancashire for 1857.

† This is the opinion of Mr Guest in his interesting and valuable
paper " On the Early English Settlements in South Britain," published
in the " Memoirs communicated to the Annual Meeting of the Archæological Institute, held at Salisbury, July 1849 ; " 8vo, Lond. 1851;
pp. 33, 34.   The other view, which has been recently put forward by
Palgrave, Lappenberg, and Kemble, may be found in D'Anville's *Etats
Formés en Europe, &c.* Par. 1771 ; p. 20.—See also Selden's *Mare
Clausum*, lib. ii. cap. 6.

ferred to and located in Britain by the Romans themselves. Upwards of forty barbarian legions, it has been reckoned, composed some of natives of Germany, some of Moors, Dalmatians, and Thracians, after having served their time in the armies of the empire, were settled and put in possession of lands in various parts of the island, principally upon the north-eastern coast, and in the neighbourhood of the Roman walls (Palgrave's *History of the Anglo-Saxons*, 1838, p. 20). But these small bodies must have soon melted into the surrounding population, and can neither have preserved their own dialects nor produced any distinguishable effect upon the general language of the country.

IV. The Third fact, and the most important of all, is, that, after the extinction of the Roman dominion, the country was in great part conquered, taken possession of, and occupied by certain tribes of Gothic race and language, whose descendants have ever since formed the bulk of its population.

THE commonly received account rests principally upon the authority of the *Historia Ecclesiastica* of Beda, who was born at Jarrow, in the bishopric of Durham, A.D. 673, and died A.D. 735. Beda makes the invaders, to whom he gives the general name of Angles or Saxons (*Anglorum sive Saxonum gens*), to have consisted of three nations or tribes, properly distinguished as the *Saxons*, the *Angles*, and the *Jutes* (or *Vitæ*).*

The Saxons, he says, came from that region in Germany which was in his own day known by the name of the country of the Old Saxons; that is, the modern Duchy of Holstein, or the country between the Elbe and the Eider. The Angles he brings from a district immediately to the north of that occupied by the Saxons; from his account, combined with others, the native country of the Angles has been supposed to have

---

* Dr Smith, in his note to Beda, *Hist. Eccles.* I. 15, seems to say that *Vitæ* is the reading of all the MSS.:—" Omnes librariorum, qui *Vitas* volunt, conatus." Yet Camden, quoting this very passage (*Britannia*, Gibson's translation, 1722, I. clviii.), expressly affirms that the MS. reading is not *Vitæ*, but *Gutæ*. The editors of the *Monumenta Britannica*, adopting *Juti* in the text, give *Vitæ* as the MS. reading in the notes to two passages (I. 15 and IV. 16); but at a third passage (also in IV. 16) no other reading than *Juti* is noted.

been the part of the Duchy of Sleswig, still bearing the
name of Angel or Angeln, lying between the Eider and
the arm of the Baltic called, after the town at its extrem-
ity, the Flensborg Wyck, or Fiorde. Beda says this district was reported to have remained uninhabited (*desertus*)
ever since the invasion. The original country of the Jutes
he places immediately to the north of that of the Angles,
by which he may mean merely the upper part of Sleswig, which is still also called South Jutland, although
commonly the name Jutland is now restricted to the
portion of the peninsula anciently known as North Jutland.

Beda is not quite consistent with other authorities, nor
even with himself, in regard to the dates at which these
several invading tribes arrived. The chronology which
has been commonly deduced from his various statements
is, that the Jutes came first, under the brothers Hengst
and Hors, or Hengist and Horsa, in A.D. 449, or rather
450 ; next the first division of the Saxons, under Ella, in
477, and the second, under Cerdic, in 495 ; then the first
body of the Angles in 527, but their principal host, under
the command of Ida, not till 547. Mr Hardy, however,
the learned editor of the *Monumenta Historica Britannica*
(Chronological Abstract, 143), prefers the computation
in the *Historia Britonum* of Nennius (a writer of the
ninth century), according to which the arrival of Hengist
and Horsa and their band would be in A.D. 428.* This

---

* Gildas (10, 11) and Nennius (23) both state that, when Clemens
Maximus revolted against the Emperor Gratian, he carried over with
him to the continent all the military force then in Britain, and that
these soldiers never returned, but settled in Armorica (Bretagne). This
was in A.D. 383. We know, however, that long after this, in A.D. 407,
the Roman army in Britain was powerful enough to set up, one after
another, three pretenders to the empire, Marcus, Gratian, and Con-

is a point of little or no importance for our present purpose. But, supposing the three tribes to have spoken, as
they probably did, different dialects, it becomes very im-
stantine. In a subsequent passage (27) Nennius speaks of the Roman
generals (*duces Romanorum*) having been on three several occasions
(*tribus vicibus*) put to death by the Britons. Yet, after all this, it is
added, the latter sought the help of the Romans against the Picts and
Scots, and, having sworn submission, had an army sent to them. Gildas (12, 14), and Beda, who follows and amplifies his account (*Hist.* i.
12, 13), make three successive embassies to have been sent to Rome,
the first and second of which were each successful in obtaining such as-
sistance as sufficed to repel the barbarians for the time; but the third,
addressed to the Consul Aetius, proved ineffectual. From what Beda
says here, and with more precision in his tract *De Sex Aetatibus Sæculi*,
the first and second of these embassies would appear to have been despatched between A.D. 414 and 419, the third in 446. The force,
therefore, which was accorded in compliance with the second embassy,
and which would, according to this version of the story, be the last
Roman force that visited the island, may very well have left in the year
418, as asserted in the National Chronicle, and by Ethelwerd. (See
ante, p. 8.) Beda states the first arrival of the Saxons to have taken
place in the first year of the reign of the Emperor Marcian, which was
A.D. 450, although he seems to have taken it for 449. There is no dispute about the date of the third embassy, in 446; but Mr Hardy supposes the first to have been despatched probably in 396, and the second
in 435, assigning the arrival of the Saxons, as stated in the text, to the
year 428 in the intervening space. This is also the date that is adopted
by Camden, who is followed, among others, by D'Anville, *Etats Formés
en Europe*, pp. 199, 200. But see the objections stated by Gibson (in
part after Stillingfleet and Usher), *Britannia*, translation of, (1722),
pp. clx. and clxi.

Consult upon the history of Roman Britain Lappenberg's *England
under the Anglo-Saxon Kings*, translated by Thorpe (2 vols. 8vo, Lond.
1845), I. 6—73; the Hon. Algernon Herbert's *Britannia after the
Romans*, 2 vols. 4to, Lond. 1836 and 1841, and his Annotations to the
edition of the *Irish Translation of Nennius*, printed by the Irish
Archæological Society, 4to, Dub. 1848; the Rev. J. C. Bruce's *Roman
Wall*, 8vo, Lond. 1851; and Mr Guest's paper in the 1851 volume of
the *Memoirs of the Archæological Institute*, already referred to. And

portant, in tracing the origin and history of the common language which grew up among them, to understand in what parts of their new country they severally settled. The accepted account of this matter derived from Beda and other sources, is, that the Jutes occupied Kent and the Isle of Wight, with part of the opposite coast of Hampshire; that the Saxons established themselves in all the rest of the country to the south of the Thames and of the Bristol Avon, and also in Essex and Middlesex, and the southern part of Hertford; and that the Angles took possession of all the rest of England, which also received its name (originally *Aengla-land,* or *Engla-land*) from them, their dominion extending, apparently, as far north as to the Forth and the Clyde. The various bodies of the old Celtic population, however, maintained their independence in the kingdoms or principalities of Strath-Clyde (or Reged, that is, *the* Kingdom), Cumbria (or Cumberland), North and South Wales (Cambria), and Cornwall, along the whole line of the western coast.

There is little doubt that among the invaders there must also have been a considerable proportion of Frisians, either from the Greater Friesland (*Frisia Major*), formerly extending from the Scheld to the Weser, or from the Lesser Friesland (*Frisia Minor*), lying on the western coast of Sleswig, opposite to the Isle of North-Strand, whence these northern Frieslanders were called *Strand-frisii*. Beda himself, in another place (*Hist. Eccles.* v. 9), enumerates the *Fresones* among the nations from whom the Angles or Saxons inhabiting Britain are known to have derived their origin. Sir Francis Palgrave goes the length of saying (*Hist. Anglo-Sax.* 33, 34), that " the

upon the general subject of the Romans in Britain, see an interesting article in the *Edinburgh Review*, No. 191 (for July 1851), pp. 177—204.

tribes by whom Britain was invaded appear principally
to have proceeded from the country now called Fries-
land; for, of all the continental dialects, the ancient
Frisick is the one which approaches most nearly to the
Anglo-Saxon of our ancestors."—(See also his " Rise and
Progress of the Eng. Commonwealth," 41, 42.)

The whole account preserved by Beda of the invasion
of Britain by the Angles, Saxons, and Jutes has been
treated as of scarcely any historical value by Mr Kemble
in his work entitled "The Saxons in England," 2 vols.
8vo, 1849 (see vol. I. pp. 1—34). But, whatever force
may be allowed to the reasoning by which Mr Kemble
would establish, on the one hand, the mixture of poetical
or fabulous elements in the narrative, and, on the other,
its unauthorised character for the greater part, it seems
very unlikely that it can be wholly without foundation
in so far as respects the only portion of it with which we
are here concerned, namely, that comprising the descent
of the invaders from a diversity of tribes, the locations of
the different tribes in the conquered country, and also
the districts on the Continent whence they had severally
come. Some distinction between the Saxons and Angles,
indeed, is sufficiently attested by the existence of those
two general appellations, to say nothing of those of
such particular states or districts as Essex, Sussex,
Wessex, East Anglia, &c. In discriminating the Saxon
and Anglian populations, Beda was dealing with facts
lying under his eye, and as to which he could hardly be
mistaken, more especially if, as is nearly certain, the
original difference of descent was still marked by a dialectic difference of speech. And, perhaps, this may not
have been the only difference that divided, and always
had divided, the Anglian and Saxon states. Nor would

two distinct and possibly rival populations, set down beside one another in a new country, readily lose the memory of their original seats. Indeed, it hardly can be seriously made matter of dispute that the Angles and Saxons of Britain were offshoots from the *Angli* and *Saxones* of the Continent :—the *Angli*, who are first mentioned by Tacitus in the first century ; the *Saxones*, who are first mentioned (at least under that name) in the second century by Ptolemy.

With regard to the Jutes, however, the case is not so clear. In the third edition of his work on the *English Language* (London, 1851), Dr Latham (pp. 10—12) has endeavoured to show that, although Jutland in Denmark undoubtedly took its name from a people called the Jutes, the derivation of any part of the invaders of Britain, after the fall of the Roman Empire, from that people, is a mistake arising from Beda (whose name for them, as we have seen, appears to be, not *Juti*, but *Vitæ*), or, it may be, some preceding writer whom he copied, having confounded the Celtic element *Wiht* in *Wiht-saetan* (the Wight-people, or inhabitants of the Isle of Wight) with the similar element in *Vit-land*, or *With-land*, which are other forms of the name of the peninsula commonly called *Jutland*.

It has been usual, also, with modern writers to assume that the continental region from which the distinctively Saxon portion of the invaders of Britain was derived was not confined to Beda's Old Saxony, or the district now called Holstein, but probably extended as far westward along the coast of the North Sea as to the Weser, or even to the Rhine.

c

V. The Fourth fact is, that in the latter part of the
ninth century extensive settlements were effected
in the North-eastern parts of England by a Scandinavian people, the Northmen or Danes.

WHATEVER may be the origin or etymological meaning
of the term *Danes*, it had come by the eighth century to
be the common name for those bands of piratical rovers,
from the countries around the Baltic, who were otherwise
called Northmen or Normans.   They are held to have
been drawn from every part of the extensive region which
the ancients designated Scandinavia; but it is remarkable
that, whereas that appellation is understood in its strictest
sense to include only the modern Sweden and Norway,
it is to Denmark that the Danes have left their name.
The geographical position of Denmark, divided from the
proper Scandinavian countries by so considerable an extent of sea, will hardly allow us to interpret the name as
signifying the Border land of the Danes, taking *mark*
here in the same sense which it has in the names of the
Anglian kingdom of *Mercia* (bordering on Wales), the
old French country of *La Marche* (bordering on Limou-
sin), and the *Mark* of the Germans, and the *Marca* of the
Italians, in various instances.   In other cases, however,
mark must be understood as meaning merely a district or
territory markéd off, or simply what we commonly call a
land or country.
It is further worth noticing that the modern kingdom
of Denmark comprehends all the districts from which
issued, according to the old accounts, the several tribes

who invaded Britain upon the fall of the Roman empire. And the *Danes* proper (who may be considered to represent the Jutes); the *Angles*, who live between the Bight of Flensborg and the river Schley on the Baltic; the *Frisons*, who inhabit the islands along the west coast of Jutland, with a part of the bailiwick of Husum in Sleswig; and the *Germans* of Holstein (Beda's Old Saxons) are still all recognised by geographers and ethnographers as distinct races (See *Universal Geography* of Malte-Brun and Balbi, English translation, p. 478).

The Latin mediæval chroniclers, under whatever notion, often speak of the Danes by the name of *Daci*, or Dacians.

The earliest notice of the appearance of the Danes in England occurs in the National Chronicle under the year 787. The passage is as follows:—Her nom Beorhtric cyning Offan dohtor Eadburhge to wive. And on his dagum cuomon aerest 3 scipu Northmanna of Haeretha lande. And tha se gerefa thaerto rad, and hie wolde drifan to thaes cyninges tune, thy he nyste hwaet hie waeron; and hiene mon thaer ofslog. Thaet waeron tha aerestan scipu Deniscra monna the Eangelcynnes lond gesohton." That is:—"This year took King Beorhtric [of Wessex] King Offa's daughter Eadburhge to wife. And in his days came first three ships of Northmen from Haeretha land.* And then the reeve thereto rode; and them would have driven to the king's town, because he wist not what they were; and him they there slew. These were the first ships of Danish men that sought the land of the English race."

* The word *Haeretha*, I believe, is not elsewhere found. It might almost be suspected to be a perversion or corruption of *Haethena* (of the Heathen). A common name for the Danes, with the Latin chroniclers, is *Gentiles*, or *Pagani*.

In 867 the Danes made themselves masters of all the eastern portion of the kingdom of Northumbria, comprising the modern counties of Northumberland, Durham, and York, and also, in part, of Cumberland, Westmoreland, and Lancashire, along the western coast. This conquest was speedily followed by the acquisition of many of the principal towns in Mercia (or the Midland Counties); which, along with East Anglia and the former kingdoms of Kent and Sussex, had for some time acknowledged the sovereignty of the King of Wessex, now beginning to be looked up to, in virtue of this extended dominion, as the supreme ruler of England. East Anglia (comprising Norfolk, Suffolk, and Cambridge) was next attacked; then Wessex itself; and at last, in the year 878, King Alfred was glad to conclude the war by a treaty with Godrum, or Guthrun, the Danish king or chief, by which he consented to cede to the invaders all the country lying along the eastern coast from the Humber to the Thames. Here accordingly, and in their conquered kingdom of Northumbria, farther to the north, these foreigners settled, probably in considerable numbers, and, although acknowledging themselves the subjects of the English king, were governed by their own laws; so that this part of the kingdom came from henceforth to be known by the name of the *Danelagh* (or Dane-law).

Finally, in 1013 the conquest of all England was effected by the Danish king Sweyn; and the crown continued in the possession of his descendants till 1042. During all this space, however, it is to be observed, the laws continued to be promulgated for the English in their own tongue. Nor is there any reason for supposing that the Danes generally ever extended their occupation of the country beyond the limits of the territory made over or abandoned to them in the reign of Alfred.

VI. The Fifth fact, and the one next in importance to the Third, is, that in the middle of the eleventh century England was conquered by the Normans, who were Danes by origin, but had been settled in France for about a century and a half, and had by this time exchanged their ancestral Scandinavian tongue for the Neo-Latin tongue called French.

A BODY of Danes, or Northmen, under their leader Hrolf, or Rollo, surnamed *the Ganger* (whatever may have been intended to be expressed by that epithet), after an unsuccessful attempt to make good a footing in England, had, a few years before Guthrun and his followers obtained their cession of territory from King Alfred, turned to the opposite coast of France, and effected their first descent in the province which at last, in 912, was yielded up to them by King Charles the Third, styled the Simple, and thereupon received the name of Normandy, which it retains to this day.

The cession of Normandy to Rollo by Charles the Simple would seem to have been a transaction very much of the same kind with the cession of the Danelagh to Guthrun by Alfred the Great. But, while the Northmen of England, after the death of Guthrun, appear to have been left without a head of their own race, those of France preserved at least the form of a distinct nationality under the descendants of Rollo, who continued to rule over the territory which their ancestor had acquired as all but independent sovereigns, with the title of Earls, Marquesses, or Dukes of Normandy.

It is probable, nevertheless, that the intermixture of

the French Northmen with the previous population of their new country may have been fully as great as in the case of the Danes settled in England. We know that both alike, after a few generations, dropped the use of the language of their ancestors, and adopted that of the nation in the midst of which they had set themselves down. This was a much greater change for the Normans of France than for the English Danes; for the Norse and Anglian were tongues of the same Gothic stock, whatever may have been their dialectic, or little more than dialectic, differences; whereas the French was a tongue, as will be presently explained, of quite another descent.

The comparatively near relationship between the languages of the English and the Danes must have facilitated and hastened that amalgamation of the two races, or absorption of the one into the other, which appears to have been completed before the next political revolution that the country underwent.

This was its conquest by the French Normans in the year 1066, under their Duke William the Second, who thereupon took the title of William the First of England, and the designation of the Conqueror. He was the seventh Duke of Normandy, and the fifth in descent from Rollo. With the Norman king and court, and a numerous following of nobility, landowners, and soldiers, established in England by this revolution, was imported and extensively introduced into use the language spoken by the Normans, which, as has been just stated, was by this time French.

The French is one of what are called the Romance or Neo-Latin tongues, by which terms are meant those corrupted forms of Latin that, in Italy and other countries, especially France and Spain, which had long been Roman provinces, were employed after the fall of the Western

Empire, first as the spoken and ultimately also as the literary languages. The names, however, of *France* and *French* have been given to the country formerly called Gaul, and to its general population and this their Neo-Latin speech, from its having been conquered in the latter part of the fifth century by a German people (or rather confederacy of various tribes), called the Franks, who spoke, of course, a Germanic or Teutonic, that is a Gothic, language. The proper language of the Franks is distinguished in modern philology from the French by being termed the *Francic*, or *Frankish*.

There were formerly two great dialects of the French language: that spoken to the south of the Loire, called the *Langue d'Oc* (or by modern philologists the *Occitanian*); and that spoken to the north of the Loire, called the *Langue d'Oyl*. *Oc* and *Oyl* (the latter now vocalised into *Oui*, and probably a corruption of *Volo*) were the words expressive of assent, or answering to our *Yes*, in the two dialects. The French brought over to England by the Normans was a form of the *Langue d'Oyl;* and it is out of that dialect chiefly that the present standard French has grown. Its great literary cultivators were the poets known as the *Trouvères* (from *trouver*, to find or invent). The poets, again, of the south of France were denominated *Troubadours*, which is merely the form of the same word proper to the southern dialect, often called the *Provençal* tongue, from the poets who composed in it in the age of its glory (the twelfth century) having been mostly patronised at the court of the Counts of Provence (first at Arles in that province, afterwards at Toulouse in Languedoc). It still subsists as a living tongue, though in ruins, and degraded to the condition of a *patois*, or merely rustic and unwritten dialect, or, rather, of a number of such dialects.

Although, however, it was the Northern French that was brought over at the Norman Conquest, the Provençal language and literature were also made familiar in England after another century by the accession to the crown (in 1154) of Henry (Plantagenet), Earl of Anjou, as Henry II., whose marriage with Eleanor of Poitou had made him master of Poitou and Guienne in the south-west of France, in addition to Normandy and his paternal domains of Anjou, Maine, and Touraine. Several Provençal compositions are attributed to his son and successor, Richard the First.

VII. It would thus appear that the languages which have been imported into and established in England by the successive populations that have conquered or settled in it, and which may each, therefore, have in a greater or less degree contributed to the formation of its existing language, belong to three several branches of the Indo-European Family; the Celtic, the Gothic, and the Classical.

WHAT is called the Indo-European family of languages may be conveniently considered as distributed into the following branches:—

1. The Sanscrit, including all the Asiatic tongues which appear to be derived from the Sanscrit, or from the Zend (the language of the ancient Persians, or, rather, of the Medes). This is sometimes called the Iranian or Arian branch, from *Iran*, the native name of Persia, of which *Aria* and *Ariana* appear to be other forms which came latterly to be commonly applied to particular provinces of the empire.

2. The Celtic.

3. The Classical, comprising the Greek and the Latin, with their modern derivatives, the Romance tongues of Italy, France, and Spain.

4. The Gothic.

5. The Slavonic, or Sarmatian (under which may be included, not only the languages of the Russians, Poles, Bohemians, and other proper Slaves, but also the Old Prussian, and the dialects of Lithuania

and Courland, which are known by the names of
the Lettonian or Lettish, and the Curonian or
Livonian).

The term *Indo-European* has been substituted for *Indo-
Germanic* since it has come to be generally admitted that
the Celtic languages belong to this family.

It will be seen from what has been stated that in investi-
gating the immediate sources of the English tongue we
have nothing to do with either the Iranian or the Sarmatian branch of the Indo-European family.

VIII. But the facts constituting the External or Historical Evidence that we have regarding the sources of the language leave us nearly altogether uninformed as to the proportionate amount of each of its several probable ingredients, and as to the precise results that have been produced by their intermixture. This we can only learn from the Internal Evidence, or that afforded by the language itself.

WHENEVER two or more populations, speaking different languages, are placed alongside of one another, under the same government, there arises a tendency, which, sooner or later, will, to a greater or less extent, become operative, towards the establishment of uniformity of speech. No such tendency arises in the case of contiguous populations living under different governments. The result of such a competition of any two languages will depend partly upon the genius and circumstances of the languages, partly upon those of the populations speaking them. This is, probably, all the length that we can safely go in stating the general law. The languages will be distinguished from each other in respect of their comparative states or advancement and cultivation, the facility with which they may be acquired (which, again, may vary with the acquirers), the degree of tenacity and affection with which they are clung to (depending, it may be, upon their inherent qualities, it may be upon merely their history and fortunes, or those of the races by whom they are spoken), and the attractions which they hold out, either by their natural beauty and capabilities, their expressiveness, their convenience or importance politically, commercially, or for general purposes, or the amount and value of their literary stores. The populations speaking them will be distinguished by their comparative numbers, by the political relation in which they stand to each other, by their respective social conditions, and even by the disposition of each, on the one hand to adopt new customs, or on the other to impose its own laws and usages upon its neighbours. The result, therefore, it is manifest, may be infinitely modified, both in itself and in the manner in which it is brought about.

The following cases, among others, may be considered:—

The retention of their proper language by the Greeks throughout all the vicissitudes of their history.

The establishment of the Latin language in Gaul and several other countries after their conquest by the Romans.

The imposition of their own language by the Turks in those portions of their empire that were earliest wrested from the Christians.

The substitution of the Arabic for the old languages in Egypt and the other Mahometan countries along the northern coast of Africa.

The substitution, after the overthrow of the Roman empire, in some of its provinces of a Gothic, in others of a semi-Gothic, speech, in place of the Latin.

The abandonment of their ancestral languages by the Franks, after their conquest of Gaul; by the Normans, after their settlement in England; and by the Manchoos, after their conquest of China.

The retention of their ancestral language by the Angles and Saxons after their conquest of Britain.

When one of two competing languages completely gives way and disappears before the other, that result is always preceded by both languages having been generally spoken for a considerable period by the population that is destined to relinquish its ancestral speech, and by at least one generation of that population having grown up in the knowledge and use of both languages from childhood. It is only a language which it has itself acquired in childhood that one generation will ever transmit to another.

But in some cases, when two languages come into competition, the one does not retire and altogether disappear before the other, but a combination takes place between them; or, if one of them acquires the ascendancy, it is still more or less modified by the other.

It is probable that some languages are naturally more impressible by a foreign element or influence than others. And the same language will vary in its impressibility at different stages of its growth, or according to the temper or circumstances of the population speaking it. It will also be more apt to be affected by the contact of one foreign language than of another.

Most commonly the effect produced by one language upon another is confined to the vocabulary. It is very rarely, if ever, that two distinct grammatical structures become intermixed; although sometimes, perhaps, a language may suffer some derangement of its grammar from coming into collision with another language.*

* See some good observations upon this subject in the late M. Fauriel's "Dante, et les Origines de la Langue et de la Littérature Italliennes" (Paris, 1854); tom. ii., pp. 409, et seq.

IX. The number of words which the English language appears to have derived from the Celtic of the original Britons, or their descendants the Welsh, is considerable; but they are scattered and unconnected, and do not constitute a distinguishable department of its vocabulary. No stream of words has flowed into it from that quarter. There has been no chemical combination of the two languages; only a mechanical intermixture to a certain extent.

THE most elaborate investigation that the question of the amount of Celtic in English has received is contained in a paper read before the Philological Society in 1844 by the late Rev. Richard Garnett, and published in the Society's *Proceedings*, vol. i. pp. 169—180.

Mr Garnett enumerates about two hundred English words (some of them, however, only provincial), which he conceives to have been borrowed from the Welsh, and he affirms that twenty times as many might be produced. Among those which he instances are the following: *funnel*, from *ffynel*, literally, an air-hole; *garter*, from *gar tas*, a shank tie; *kick*, from *cic*, the foot; *cuts*, in the expression "to draw cuts," from *cwtws*, a lot; to *wed*, from *gweddu*, to yoke; *bride*, from *priawd*, meaning one won and possessed.

The word *leather* Mr Garnett gives as an instance of a term which is found in many Teutonic (or Gothic) as well as in all the Celtic dialects, but which there are, nevertheless, reasons for believing to be originally Celtic, in which class of languages alone its proper or primary meaning is to be detected. The Celtic term (*lled* in Welsh, and *leathan* in Gaelic) signifies *flat* or *broad.**

---

* Another of Mr Garnett's instances is the word *mutton.* This word we have, doubtless, received immediately from the French *mouton*, anciently *moulton ;* its termination being the common augmentative *one* of the modern Italian, in which language the word assumes the form of *montone.* But its emphatic portion, *mut, mont,* or *moult,* is found in all the leading Celtic tongues ; it is *mollt* in Welsh and Irish, *mult* in Gaelic, *moltz* in Cornish, and *maut* in Armorican. A curious theory with regard to this element has been started by Mr Grant of Corrimony, in his " Thoughts on the Origin and Descent of the Gael," 8vo, Lond. 1827 ; he contends that it is identical with the Latin *multa*, or *mulcta,* the legal term for a pecuniary penalty, whence we have our English *mulct*, with the same meaning. There can be little doubt that the *c* has been inserted only to distinguish the word from the feminine of *multus ;* and the common explanations, therefore, connecting it either with *mulceo* or with *mulco* (founded mainly upon the presence of that letter) may be at once dismissed. If it is to be regarded as identical with the *multa* of *multus,* its true signification is probably *numbered* or *counted ;* and this view has the advantage of explaining the adjective also. It is nearly that taken by the learned Joseph Scaliger, who, in his Commentary on Varro, makes it an obsolete imperative of the same signification with *numera.* Varro himself, in his work on the Latin Language (De Lingua Latina, *iv.* 36), conjectures that it must be an old form of *una.* On the other hand, the following passages from the Elder Pliny (writing in the first century of our era), and from Aulus Gellius (in the second), seem to lend considerable support to the view taken by Mr Grant : —" *Pecunia* ipsa a *pecore* appellatur.......*Multatio* quoque non nisi *ovium* boumque impendio dicebatur : non omittenda priscarum legum benevolentia ; *cautum quippe est, ne bovem priusquam ovem nominaret qui indiceret multam.*"—*Plin. Nat. His. xviii.* 3. "*Multa quæ* appellatur suprema instituta est in singulos duarum ovium, boum triginta ; pro copia scilicet boum, proque ovium penuria.......*Minima multa est ovis unius...* .... Quando igitur nunc quoque a magistratibus populi Romani more

Some existing English words are historically recorded to have been originally Celtic. One instance is the word *basket*, which is spoken of as having been a British word both by Juvenal (*Sat. xii.* 46) and by Martial (*Epig. xiv.* 99). Its Welsh form is *bassgawd*, apparently from *basc* or *basg*, an interweaving or netting. But it may still, perhaps, be questioned whether it was introduced into the English directly from the Welsh, or through the medium of the Latin.

It is argued by Mr. Garnett that the borrowing by the English from the Britons of such words as this, significant of articles or of arts and processes with which they had been previously unacquainted, is a thing in itself likely to have happened. In other cases, he thinks, the new-comers may have been led to adopt a Celtic word now and then from its mere oddity. In illustration of this he quotes the word *bother*, which is commonly stated to be only another form of *pother*, no further account being given of either, but which Mr Garnett holds to be a Celtic term often occurring in the Irish translation of the Scriptures in the sense of "to be grieved or troubled in mind." But it may perhaps be suspected that *pother*, at any rate, whatever may be the case with *bother*, is rather

majorum multa dicitur, vel minima vel suprema, *observari solet ut oves genere virili appellentur.* Atque ita M. Varro verba hœc legitima, quibus minima multa diceretur, concepit:—'M. Terentius, quando citatus neque respondet neque excusatus est, *Ego ei unum ovem multam dico.' Ac, nisi eo genere diceretur, negaverunt justam videri multam.''—Aul. Gell. Noct. Att. xi.* 1. It is remarkable, that, as the penalty designated *multa* was, it would thus appear, understood by the Romans to be in some way or other, though nobody could tell how, connected not only with a sheep, but specially with a male sheep, so the latter, or more strictly a *vervex*, or wether, is the kind of sheep which the Celtic terms properly denote.

connected with the German *poltern*, to make a noise, to bluster, and *gepolter*, a rumbling noise.*

It is to be remembered, in the consideration of this question, that, diverse and almost hostile as the Celtic and Gothic forms of speech are, they are still both branches of the same Indo-European family, and that they must have radically much in common. In the Latin language, too, from which the English has derived so large a portion of its vocabulary in later stages, there are both a Celtic and a Gothic element.

A late French writer, Mons. W. F. Edwards, in a work entitled "Recherches sur les Langues Celtiques," 8vo, Paris, 1844, has (pp. 11—13) attempted to show that certain existing peculiarities of English pronunciation are to be attributed to the contact and action of the Welsh language.

The two principal subsisting Celtic languages are the Welsh and the Irish: the Cornish and the Breton, or Armorican, being subordinate varieties of the former; the Scottish Gaelic and the Manks (or dialect of the Isle of Man), of the latter.

* But in Shakespeare we have the word in a somewhat different form :—

> "Let the great gods,
> That keep this dreadful *pudder* o'er our heads,
> Find out their enemies now."—*Lear*, iii. 2.

This is the reading of all the Folios. The first Quarto (1608), however, has *powther*.

X. There are scarcely to be found any words in our present English which it can be supposed to have inherited from the Latin spoken by the Roman colonists who had preceded the Angles and Saxons in the dominion, and, to a great extent, in the occupation, of the country. Almost the only words of Latin origin that had established themselves in the language before the Norman Conquest are a few which it had received from the Roman ecclesiastics, whose visits commenced at the close of the sixth century, or from books.

SUCH Latin ingredient as the English language may contain, derived from the speech of a portion of the population when the country was a province of the Roman empire, has been designated the *Latin of the First Period*. But it can hardly be said to exist. The only fragments or vestiges of it that have been instanced are the *caster, cester, chester*, and whatever other variations they may be of the Latin *castra* (a camp) preserved in such names of places as Lancaster, Manchester, Leicester, &c.; the *coln* of Lincoln, and a few other towns, an abridgment or corruption of *colonia* (a colony); and the word *street*, from *stratum* or *strata*. But this last is probably as much a Gothic as a Latin word.

What of the Latin language of Britain survived the imperial dominion would appear to have been preserved only in the Celtic of Wales. But it is still an unsettled question how much of Latin there is in the Welsh.

The Latin ingredient introduced into the English language by the Roman churchmen, and by the learning which they imported, has been distinguished as the *Latin of the Second Period.* Attention was first directed to this part of the language by Mr Guest, who, in his "History of English Rhythms" (2 vols. 8vo, Lond. 1838, vol. ii. pp. 108, 109), has instanced the following Latin words, among others, as found in manuscripts of a very early date:—*Mynster* (from *monasterium*), a minster or monastery; *portic* (from *porticus*), a porch; *cluster* (from *claustrum*), a cloister; *munuc* (from *monachus*), a monk; *bisceop* (from *episcopus*), a bishop; *sanct* (from *sanctus*), a saint; *calic* (from *calix*), a chalice; *prædician* (from *prædicare*), to preach; *leon* (from *leo*), the lion; *peterselige* (from *petroselinum*), parsley; *pipor* (from *piper*), pepper; &c.

Mr Guest observes that the Latin terms introduced into the English at this stage of the language are nearly all *concrete* terms (or significant of things), whereas those introduced at a later date are mostly *abstract* (or significant of notions).

It may be added, that in most of the instances mentioned above the modern English word is not a modification of the original formation, but a new formation obtained either directly from the Latin or through the medium of the French. This is evidently the case with *monastery, porch* (Fr. *porche*), *cloister* (old Fr. *cloistre*), *saint* (Fr. *saint*), *preach* (Fr. *prêcher*), *lion* (Fr. *lion*), *parsley* (Fr. *persil*).

XI. It has not yet been clearly proved that any con
siderable part of the standard form of the English
language is, in its origin, Scandinavian as distinguished from Germanic ; though a Scandinavian
element appears to be more or less recognisable in
some of the provincial dialects, and farther investigation may probably show that its influence has
been more extensive than has hitherto been generally supposed.

THE Gothic branch of the Indo-European Family of
Languages may be conveniently distributed into the following subdivisions :—

1. The Mœso-Gothic (the language spoken by the
Goths, who, about A. D. 376, were permitted by
the Emperor Valens to occupy the Lower Mœsia,
now Bulgaria, near the mouth of the Danube and
on the right bank of that river, having previously
resided for at least a century on the opposite or
northern bank, and having been recently converted
to Christianity by Ulphilas, whose translation of
part of the New Testament is the only specimen
of their language that remains, being, however, the
oldest specimen that exists of any Gothic tongue).
2. The Germanic, or Teutonic (the various dialects
spoken by the German nations).
3. The Scandinavian (the various dialects spoken by
the nations settled around the Baltic, or in the
countries included by the ancients under the somewhat vague appellation of Scandinavia, and now
known as Norway, Sweden, and Denmark).

Of these subdivisions the second, or Germanic, further separates into the High Germanic and the Low Germanic (meaning the dialects or languages respectively of Southern and of Northern Germany, of which the former is a comparatively elevated, the latter a low-lying, region). The principal, or what may be called the representative, High Germanic language is what is commonly known as the German, and is called by the Germans themselves the *Hoch Deutsch*, which used to be Englished *High Dutch*. The chief exclusively Low Germanic tongue is that of Holland, to which the term *Dutch* has now come in this country to be restricted, and of which it is significant without any distinctive epithet. Ancient Germany, it is to be remembered, included the countries now known as Holland and the Netherlands.

The principal existing Scandinavian dialects, again, are the Icelandic, the Danish and Norwegian (which are nearly the same), the Ferroic, and the Swedish. The Icelandic, which is regarded as the standard Scandinavian tongue, is often called the Old Danish, or Norse; and the latter term is sometimes used, in a larger acceptation, to include all the Scandinavian dialects.

The substance of the above statement may be thus exhibited in a tabular form :—

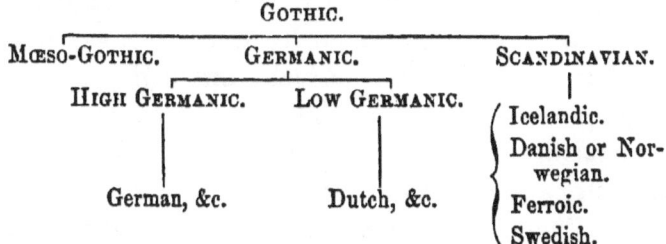

Of the Gothic invaders and conquerors of Britain in the fifth and sixth centuries, the Saxons may be admitted to have come, apparently, rather from Lower Germany than from Scandinavia. But the Continental localities assigned in the received account to the Jutes and the Angles would make them both to have been Scandinavian, at least according to modern notions. The subject, however, is surrounded with obscurity. It is questioned, as we have seen, whether there were any Jutes among the invaders. Beda's account even of the quarter whence the Angles came is disputed. Little or nothing can be gathered from the manner in which they are mentioned either by Tacitus or by Ptolemy. Finally, we do not know that the languages of the Germanic and those of the Scandinavian stock were so widely distinguished at this date as they now are.

The probability is, however, that there was a dialectic difference between the speech proper to the Saxons, distinctively so called, and that of the Angles, and also that the latter at least approximated more than the former to that of the Danes. The two facts from which these inferences may be drawn are;—the first, that certain peculiarities of a Scandinavian character are to be found in the Anglian, even of a date anterior to the first Danish occupation of a part of England in the latter half of the ninth century; the second, that the Scandinavian dialect imported by the Danish settlers and the Anglian, although it is unquestionable that they differed considerably, yet, if they were not from the first mutually intelligible, appear to have coalesced and melted into one language with much more facility than they would have done if there had not been also a near natural relationship between them.

The differences between the Anglian and the standard form of the language spoken or written in England, and the traces of Scandinavianism to be found in the former and in the provincial dialects descended from it, have been expounded by Mr Kemble and by Mr Garnett in several papers read before the Philological Society in 1844 and 1845, and printed in the second volume of the Society's *Proceedings*.

Although the Gothic conquerors of Britain were collectively called Saxons by the Celts whom they dispossessed (that having been the name by which the latter had been accustomed to know the persevering enemies from the opposite continent by whom their coasts had been so long assailed), they and their language were commonly called English, that is, Anglian, by themselves, and the country England, or the land of the Angles. This, it has been argued, would seem to indicate that the said language was probably first employed in literature, not by the Saxons Proper of the south, but by the Angles of the north. Even the political supremacy which was at last acquired by the former never was able to obliterate the appellations bestowed upon the nation and upon the language by or with reference to the latter, any more than the language spoken by the Romans ever ceased to be called Latin, either by themselves or others.

The head district of the Angles, as distinct from the Saxons, in Britain was the Kingdom of Northumbria, which in its full extent stretched from the Humber to the Frith of Forth, and included the modern counties of Northumberland, Durham, and York, with at least the eastern parts of Cumberland, Westmoreland, and Lancashire, besides all the south-east of Scotland. But East Anglia, comprehending modern Norfolk and Suffolk, with Cambridgeshire and a part of Bedfordshire, was also, as its name implies, an Anglian kingdom. So was Mercia in the main. Now these parts of the island, which had been taken possession of by the Angles in the sixth century, were also those that fell under the power of the

Danish invaders of the ninth century, and in which they
settled in considerable numbers. The *Danelagh*, as the
range of country in question came to be called from
the time of Guthrun's treaty with Alfred the Great (in
878), appears to have comprehended all East Anglia and
the greater portion of Mercia and Northumbria. The
remarkable circumstance of the Danes having thus seated
themselves exclusively in the Anglian districts cannot but
awaken a suspicion that they found in the Angles a race
more nearly related to themselves in blood and in language than the Saxons were.

Specimens of the Anglian dialect of Northumbria have
come down to us, extending certainly from the close,
possibly from the commencement, of the seventh century
to the latter part of the tenth, and therefore embracing
a considerable period both before and after the Danish
invasion. Mr Kemble arranges them in three classes:
the first, consisting of a few inscriptions upon stones,
mostly in runic characters, and of "uncertain, but probably very great, antiquity;" the second, consisting of
proper names found upon coins; the third and most important, of literary compositions. Of these last the principal are, a translation of the Psalms in one of the Cotton
Manuscripts, which has been conjectured to be possibly
as old as the beginning of the seventh century; a frag-
ment of verse attributed to the poet Caedmon, which, if
it be genuine, must be of the latter half of that century;
a hymn composed on his death-bed by Beda, who died in
the year 735; and two works which appear to belong to
the latter part of the tenth century, the one known as the
Durham Ritual, the other a *Gloss*, or literal interlined
translation, of the Latin Gospels, in what is called *St
Cuthbert's* or the *Durham Book*.

This succession of specimens of the Anglian dialect,

examined in chronological order, appears to afford evidence that the dialect, after the Danish occupation, gradually underwent certain changes which would be accounted for by the supposition of its having been subjected to the action of a Scandinavian element or influence.

The most remarkable of these changes is that of the proper termination of the infinitive *an* into the old Norse termination *a*. The form *a*, or *æ*, appears in two or three instances in one of the stone inscriptions, that on the Ruthwell Cross, which Mr Kemble, by whom it was first deciphered and explained, conjectures to be probably of the ninth century; but in the *Durham Ritual* and in *St Cuthbert's Book*, which are both of the latter part of the tenth century, the new infinitive in *a* is used in all verbs, with the exception only of the substantive verb, *bian*, to be.

Mr Garnett further adduces, in support of this theory of the gradually increased Scandinavianisation of the Anglian dialect under the contagion of that of the Danish settlers, the evidence afforded by certain specimens of the Northumbrian English of the fourteenth century, and also various peculiar forms and vocables still retained in the speech of the northern counties.

The topographical nomenclature of the country occupied by the Danes is to this day partially Scandinavian. It is known historically, indeed, that they gave their present names to the towns of Derby and Whitby, the terminating syllable of which is the Norse form of the word for a town (otherwise *wic*, or *wich*, as in many English names, or *vic*, as in the Latin *vic-us*), and the same which makes part of the compound *bye-laws* (properly the laws of the town as distinguished from the general laws of the realm).

In the twelfth century Giraldus Cambrensis, and in the thirteenth John of Wallingford, speak of both the

population and the language of the northern parts of
England as still bearing manifest traces of a Danish
origin. And in the middle of the fourteenth century
Higden, after having mentioned the mixture of the original
English, first with the Danes, and then with the Normans,
adds, that the whole speech of the Northumbrians, especially in Yorkshire, was so harsh and rude that the southern men, of whom he himself was one, could hardly understand it.

It is generally admitted that, whatever may be the
case with the standard English, several of its provincial
dialects still exhibit more or less of a Danish or Scandinavian element. Dr Latham (*English Language*, third
edit. pp. 551, &c.), while he regards the Lowland Scotch
as being " probably more Danish than any South British
dialect," describes the Danish admixture as very great in
the dialect of Northumberland, as considerable in the
dialects of the North and part of the West Riding of
Yorkshire, at its minimum in those of Shropshire, Stafford-
shire, and West Derbyshire ; the language of Lincolnshire
he characterises as only " not Danish in proportion to the
other signs of Scandinavian intermixture to be found in
the district, such as the prevalence of the Danish termination *by* in the names of towns, the Danish traditions,
and the Danish physiognomy of the people ; " and the
language of the old metrical romance of " Havelok the
Dane," the subject of which is a Lincolnshire tradition,
he declares to be " preëminently Danish."

Mr Guest, nevertheless (*English Rhythms*, ii. 186—207),
finds traces of Danish " neither in our MSS. nor in our
dialects." He admits, indeed, that there may possibly be
something of the kind in the language of certain parts
of the British islands which were " wholly peopled with
Northmen—as the Orkneys, Caithness, and much of the

eastern coast north of Forth;" but, as for the vestiges
of Dano-English commonly produced, he observes that
"these may be found in districts where the Northman
never settled, and are missing from counties where he
certainly did;" and he argues that the peculiarities which
have always distinguished northern from southern English
are to be sufficiently accounted for by the fact of the
Angles having, before they left the continent, been the
neighbours of the Danes. At the same time he holds
that the language brought over by the Danes who settled
in the country in the ninth century cannot have differed
very much from English—that it must have been "little
more than an English dialect." But is this likely after
a separation of more than three centuries, even if the two
languages had been previously ever so nearly related?

In an article on the "Saxon Language and Literature"
in the *Penny Cyclopædia* (published in 1841), Mr Guest
refers to the *Gloss* in *St. Cuthbert's Book* and to the
Durham Ritual as furnishing the strongest of all the argu-
ments against the supposed influence of the language of
the Danish settlers, inasmuch, he observes, as we have all
the peculiarities of the northern dialect in every page of the
Gloss, and in many parts of the *Ritual*, although both
were written before the Danish settlement took place.
But, as we have seen, so far is this last assumption from
being established that the *Gloss* and the *Ritual* are both
assigned by others to the latter part of the tenth century.
This is the judgment, not only of Mr Garnett and Mr
Kemble, but also, at least as to the *Ritual*, of Dr Latham
(*English Language*, 549). Nor is the *Ritual* assigned by
its editor (Mr Stevenson), as Mr Guest supposes, to the
early part of the ninth century; Mr Stevenson only ex-
presses an opinion that no part of the writing can be older
than the commencement of that century. The *Gloss*,

again, is declared in a memorandum on the MS. to have been made for a Bishop Aelfsig, who was probably either Aelfsig Bishop of Winchester from A.D. 951 to 958, or Aelfsig Bishop of Chester-le-street from 968 to 990.

"The *Sexe*," says Mr Guest (*English Rhythms*, ii. 190), "came from the south-western corner of the ancient *Ongle*, and were parted only by the Elbe from the Netherlandish races; while the *Engle*, who landed at Bamborough, came from the north-eastern coast, and were neighbours to the Dane." And to this statement he appends the following note:—"There is reason to believe that this word *Sexe* meant nothing more than *Seamen*, and that it was first given to such of the *Engle* as made piracy their trade. But after the *Sexe* settled in Britain, though, as it would seem, they sometimes called their speech *English*, their new country *Engleland*, and themselves the *Engle-kin*, yet they were, for the most part, distinguished from the Engle of the north—the phrase *Engle and Sexe* being made use of when the writer would include the entire English population of the island. That the Sexe *were* a tribe of Engle, I think there can be little doubt. Everything tends to show, that at the beginning of the fifth century there were only *four* great Gothic races in the north of Europe—the *Sweon*, the *Dene*, the *Engle*, and the *Swefe*." The *Sweon* are the *Suiones* of Tacitus, supposed to have given its name to Sweden; the *Swefe* are the *Suevi* of the ancients, held to be the same with the modern Suabians.

XII. The foreign element which has mingled to by far
the largest extent with the original substance of
the English language is that peculiar modification
of the Latin which grew up in the northern part of
what was once the Roman province of Gaul, and
which now forms the classical French.

THERE was a good deal of intercourse between England and Normandy in the reign of the last of the so-
called Saxon kings, Edward styled the Confessor, who,
when he came to the throne in the year 1042, was nearly
forty years of age, and had resided ever since his boyhood at the Norman court; for the Dukes of Normandy
were his nearest relations, he and the father of William
the Conqueror being cousins-german. He was, therefore,
notwithstanding his birth and descent by the father's
side, much more a Frenchman than an Englishman; and
we are told that he gave great offence to his subjects by
the preference which he showed for the language of
France, as well as by the number of ecclesiastics and
others whom he drew over out of that country, and appointed to offices and livings in England.

But what planted the French language in England was,
as has been already observed, the acquisition of the dominion of the country by William Duke of Normandy in
the memorable year 1066.

There is no probability in the assertion which has often
been made that the Conqueror sought to extirpate the English language, and to substitute the French in its place. He
was incapable of entertaining a project so palpably im-

practicable. So far, in fact, was he from cherishing any dislike to the language of his new subjects that he is recorded to have at first applied himself vigorously to learn English, till more pressing occupations compelled him to give up the attempt. He probably found that to conquer the language was harder work than to conquer the country at the age at which he had arrived; for he was about forty when he became king.

Among the consequences, however, of the great revolution that had taken place, were the following:—

1. A French-speaking royal family was placed upon the throne, surrounded, of course, by a French-speaking court. Even when the male line of the Conqueror died out, it was succeeded by another, that of the Plantagenets of Anjou, which was also French. It is known, in fact, that French continued to be the language in common use with every English king from the Conqueror down to Richard the Second inclusive, or to the end of the fourteenth century; it is not known that, with the exception, perhaps, of Richard the Second, any one of them ever did or could speak English.

2. A very great number of Normans, all speaking French, were brought over and settled in the kingdom. There were the military forces, by which the conquest was achieved and maintained, both those in command and the private soldiers; there was a vast body of churchmen, spread over the land, and occupying eventually every ecclesiastical office in it, from the primacy down to that of the humblest parish or chapel priest, besides half filling, probably, all the monastic establishments; there were all the officers of state and inferior civil functionaries down to nearly the lowest grade; finally, there were, with few exceptions, all the landholders, great and small, throughout the kingdom. The members of all these classes and their fami-

lies must have been at first entirely ignorant of English, and they and their descendants would naturally continue for a longer or shorter time to use only the language of their ancestors.

3. Although it may be inferred from the expressions of Ordericus Vitalis, a contemporary chronicler, that at first causes at law were pleaded in English even before the Conqueror himself,—for it was specially in order to be able to understand the pleadings without the intervention of an interpreter that William, according to that writer, set himself to study the language,—it would yet appear that French soon came to be exclusively the language of oral pleadings, at least in all the superior courts. It could not well be otherwise, while the judges in those courts were all Normans. No law or express ordinance introducing such a practice is upon record; but there is an act of the legislature, as we shall presently find, which distinctly attests the fact of its existence. Neither laws nor deeds, however, were ever drawn up in French till more than a century and a half after the Conquest; all the new laws that were promulgated were in Latin till after the accession of Edward the First (in 1272), when they began to be sometimes in Latin, sometimes in French. Even the judgments or decisions of the courts in which the pleadings were in French were not always enrolled in that language, but often in Latin. And the charters granted by the Norman kings were frequently in English down to the accession of Henry the Second (in 1154), when Latin was substituted, which had been the language uniformly employed for the same purpose by the old kings down to the time of Alfred the Great. (See Palgrave's *Rise and Progress of the English Commonwealth*, i. 56; or *Preface* to Record Commission edition of the *Statutes of*

the Realm; or *Luders's Tracts*, 8vo, *Bath*, 1810, *Tract·*
Sixth.)

The results were :—

1. That, Latin continuing to be as heretofore the
language in which all learned works were written, in
popular and fashionable literature the native language
of the country was completely supplanted by the foreign
tongue which the Normans had imported.

2. That French came to be for a time understood and
spoken extensively even by the population of English
blood.

Robert Holcot, writing in the beginning of the fourteenth century, informs us that there was no English
taught in the schools of his time, but that the first language children learned was the French, and that through
the medium of that when they went to school they
were afterwards taught Latin. This practice, he says,
was introduced at the Conquest, and had continued ever
since. The teachers, in fact, who were all churchmen,
were most of them foreigners, and altogether, or nearly
altogether, unacquainted with English. Holcot's statement is repeated by Ralph Higden about the middle of
the same century, with some additional particulars.*

---

* See the passage from Higden, as translated by Trevisa, in the
Appendix.

XIII. In the new circumstances, political and social, in which England was placed by the Norman Conquest, the old literary language of the country perished with the peculiar civilisation of which it formed a part, somewhat as did the classical Latin after the overthrow of the Western empire; but more rapidly, in consequence of the important additional disadvantage of having to encounter the rivalry of a new civilisation, and of another tongue also beginning to be employed in literature. Ceasing to be read or patronised, it ceased to be written; and, no longer written, it soon came to be no longer understood. But there was still left in use as the common or vernacular tongue a species or form of English, differing from the English that was written before the Conquest chiefly by its comparative want or neglect of inflections; and this became the germ of our modern national speech, or at least of so much of it as is of native origin.

THE only considerable composition in the original form of the English language that is known to have been written after the Norman Conquest is the portion of the *National* (or so called Saxon) *Chronicle*, extending from that event to the death of King Stephen (in 1154). Before the latter date this Original English had apparently begun to be looked upon as a dead language, and to be only studied as such by a few antiquaries, like the Latin chroniclers Florence of Worcester and Henry of Huntingdon. It is commonly designated *Saxon*, or *Anglo-Saxon*.

E

The term *Anglo-Saxon*, whether as applied to the language or to the people by whom it was spoken, must be understood to mean properly Saxon of England as distinguished from Saxon of the Continent; just as *Anglo-Norman* means Norman of England, as distinguished from Norman of the Continent. It is a compound formed on the principle of assuming *Saxon* as the name of the people and of the language, and *England* as that of the country. The Anglo-Saxon is merely one dialect of Saxon, as the Continental or Old Saxon is another. It cannot mean, as is sometimes supposed, the language of the Angles *and* Saxons.*

The following are some of the principal grammatical peculiarities in which the Original English (or *Anglo-Saxon*) differs from what is now called English:—

The nouns, both substantive and adjective, are of three genders—masculine, feminine, and neuter.

---

* Our ancestors, by whom this language was spoken, usually called their country *England* (*Engla-land* or *Anglia*), and themselves and their language *English.* These are the terms commonly used in the *Chronicle.* Beda entitles his Latin History *Historia Gentis Anglorum Ecclesiastica*, and, in enumerating the languages spoken in Britain, he designates that of the Angles and Saxons generally as *lingua Anglorum.* Sometimes, however, he has *Angli sive Saxones*, and *Anglica sive Saxonica* (*lingua*). The Latin chroniclers after the Conquest, meaning by the *English* the then mixed population and language, commonly take advantage of the term *Saxon* to distinguish the people and the language before that revolution. It may be doubted, perhaps, in what sense exactly we are to understand the *Angulsaxones* of Asser, the biographer of Alfred the Great, before the Conquest, and the *Angulsaxones*, *Angli-Saxones*, and *Anglo-Saxones* of Florence of Worcester after it,—whether, that is to say, as meaning the Saxons of England or the Angles *and* Saxons; but in modern philology, at any rate, by *Anglo-Saxon* we can only be understood to mean, as has been said the *Saxon* (or *English*) of England as distinguished from the *Old Saxon* of the Continent.

The cases are formed by variations of the termination, the terminations being:—

Sing. Nom.	*a, e, u, ow,* or a consonant.
Acc.	*e, u, ow,* or a consonant.
Dat. & Abl.	*a, e,* or a consonant (commonly *an* or *um*).
Gen.	*a, e,* or a consonant (commonly *es* or *an*).
Plur. Nom.	*a, e, u,* or a consonant (commonly *an* or *as*).
Acc.	always the same with the Nom.
Dat. & Abl.	always *um.*
Gen.	generally *a, ena,* or *ra,* sometimes *u.*

The definite article *se, seó, thaet,* is also used both as the demonstrative and as the relative pronoun. And the relative pronoun is often expressed by the indeclinable *the,* which has now come to be used as the definite article. The indefinite article was sometimes expressed by *sum* (our modern *some*), and often (as in Greek or Latin) was not expressed at all.

The personal pronouns,—*Ic* (*I*), *thú* (*thou*), *he, heó, hit* (*he, she, it*),—as well as the possessive and interrogative pronouns, are also all declined. *He* and *hit* make *his* in the genitive sing.; *heó* makes *hire:* whence evidently our *his* (down to a comparatively recent date used also as the genitive of the neuter, where we now say *its*) and *her.* Our *their* appears to be the gen. plur. *hira* (common to all the genders); as our *they* is the nom. plur. *hí.* *Him,* again, is the original dat. sing. masc. and neut., and dat. plur. in all the genders.

In the Original English verb, the infinitive ends in *an;* the present participle in *ende,* the past participle in *od,* or

ed, or *d*. The prefix *ge* is found with all parts of the
verb, but most commonly with the parts expressing past
time. In the present indicative the termination of the
2d pers. sing. is *ast* or *st*, that of the 3d pers. *ath* or *th*;
that of the plural persons *ath*. The terminations of the
singular persons of the past tense are in the indicative,
de, dest, de ; in the subjunctive, *de* throughout; so that
both tenses are completely distinguished from the past
participle passive. The plural persons in both tenses al
end in *don*.

The written form of our earliest English, it thus appears,
is, like the Greek or the Latin, what may be called an inflectional language. But we do not know that this was
the only form of the language in use even before the Conquest. In any country, the standard or literary language
of which is highly inflectional, it would seem to be only
what might be looked for, that there should exist also an
oral dialect of a less artificial character and looser texture ;
for it is found that, whatever may be the advantages of a
certain kind which an elaborate system of inflection gives
to a language, all the ordinary purposes of communication
can be sufficiently attained with very little inflection, or
even with none at all. It is remarkable that the language
which is, perhaps, the oldest in the world, the Chinese, is
also the least inflected. It is generally held, indeed, that
the Chinese has probably never passed through or reached
the inflected stage. But still the fact of its actual condition might awaken a suspicion that, perhaps, the latest
stage of language may consist in its complete emancipa-
tion from inflection and the shackles of grammar. Here,
as in other cases, the simplest form of the instrument
may be found to be the most perfect. It does not appear
that the Chinese language is found by those to whom it

is native to be, in consequence of its scanty or no grammar, deficient either in distinctness or even in rhetorical and poetical expressiveness. A few particles and other auxiliary or connecting words are stated to have made their way into the modern form of the language; but it does not appear to have acquired anything of inflection properly so called. Indeed, the acquisition or growth of inflection by a language is probably unknown as an actual phenomenon.

It has been conjectured that the Italian language, or something not very unlike the modern Italian, may have been a spoken dialect among the ancient Romans. It is possible that in the same manner each of the other Neo-Latin tongues, as they are called, may have sprung up and acquired in great part its peculiar form before the Western Empire was overthrown, and its provinces overrun, or at least taken possession of, by the northern barbarians. What is called the Romaic, or modern Greek, may be substantially a popular idiom of ancient times. The great literary language of India, the Sanscrit, has its less elaborately artificial form, the Pracrit. So may there have been, even in the best days of the written or classical Anglo-Saxon, or Original English, a spoken dialect of the language which was comparatively uninflectional; and this, preserved on the lips of the people, may have survived the Norman Conquest, when the literary language sunk before its foreign rival.

But if, as is commonly assumed, the irregular English, or Semi-Saxon, as it is commonly called, which we find to have been in use after the Conquest was a new form of speech, which had in some way or other been produced by that catastrophe,—was, in other words, the old national language in ruins,—it may be held as certain that it was not through any direct action of the French language upon it, as used to be the received explanation, that the corruption of the Original English was brought about. There is not a trace of French to be found in the supposed new dialect. Nor would an intermixture of French have produced the peculiar change which distinguishes that dialect from the old regular English, or Saxon.

It has been urged, moreover, that such a change, consisting in the breaking up of the inflectional system of the language, if it cannot be affirmed to have taken place in conformity with a tendency inherent in all languages, is at least only what has happened, in a greater or less degree, to every other language of the stock to which the Original English belongs. The first English writer by whom attention was called to this last consideration was probably the late Dr Alexander Murray, who died in 1813, though his *History of European Languages* was not given to the world till 1823. He there observes (i. 21), speaking of the change which the English language is supposed to have undergone in the period immediately subsequent to the Conquest:—"A similar process was observable, at the same time, in the kindred dialects of Holland and Germany, though exposed to no external violence. . . . . These continental tongues insensibly lost the greater part of the inflections which they inherited from antiquity." But the fullest and most distinct statement upon the whole question is that of the late Mr Price, in the Preface to his edition of Warton's *History of English Poetry* (1824, p. 109) :—"An influx of foreigners, or a constant intercourse with and dependence upon them, may corrupt the idiom of a dialect to a limited extent, or charge it with a large accumulation of exotic

terms, but this change in the external relation of the
people speaking the dialect will neither *confound* the
original elements of which it is composed nor destroy the
previous character of its grammar. The *lingua franca*,
as it is called, of the shores washed by the Mediterranean
Sea contains an admixture of words requiring all the
powers of an erudite linguist to trace the several ingredients to their parent sources; yet, with all the corruptions
and innovations to which this oddly assorted dialect has
been subjected, it invariably acknowledges the laws of
Italian grammar. A similar inundation of foreign terms
is to be found in the German writers of the seventeenth
century, where the mass of Latin, Greek, and French expressions almost exceeds the number of vernacular words;
yet here again the stranger matter has been made to
accommodate itself to the same inflections and modal
changes as those which govern the native stock. . . . . .
That some change had taken place in the style of composition and general structure of the language since the
days of Alfred, is a matter beyond dispute; but that
these mutations were a consequence of the Norman invasion, or were even accelerated by that event, is wholly
incapable of proof; and nothing is supported upon a
firmer principle of rational induction than that the same
effects would have ensued if William and his followers
had remained in their native soil. The substance of the
change is admitted on all hands to consist in the sup-
pression of those grammatical intricacies occasioned by
the inflection of nouns, the seemingly arbitrary distinctions of gender, the government of prepositions, &c.
How far this may be considered as the result of an innate
law of the language, or some general law in the organisa-
tion of those who spoke it, we may leave for the present

undecided; but that it was in no way dependent upon external circumstances is established by this undeniable fact,—that every branch of the Low German stock, from whence the Anglo-Saxon sprang, displays the same simplification of its grammar. In all these languages there has been a constant tendency to relieve themselves of that precision which chooses a fresh symbol for every shade of meaning, to lessen the amount of nice distinctions, and detect as it were a royal road to the interchange of opinion."

The assumption here proceeded upon with regard to the simplification of their grammatical structure undergone by all the languages of the Low Germanic stock has been extended by more recent writers to the Scandinavian languages of Denmark and Sweden; so that, whether the English is to be regarded as belonging exclusively to the Low Germanic or partially to the Scandinavian stock, its transition from an inflected to a comparatively uninflected condition would be accounted for upon this theory by a tendency probably inherent in its constitution.

Mr Guest, making no distinction here between what are commonly called the stages of Semi-Saxon and of Old or Early English, offers the following explanation of the way in which he conceives the transformation of the language to have been brought about (*Eng. Rhythms*, ii. 105, &c.):—" The causes which in the twelfth century gave birth to the Old English worked nearly at the same time a like change in all the kindred dialects, save the most northerly, which, safe from their influence amid the snows of Iceland and of Sweden, long retained (and indeed still retain) many of the earliest features of our language. . . A difference is always to be found between the written and the spoken language of a people. The look, the tone, the action, are means of expression which the speaker may employ, and the writer cannot; to make himself understood, the latter must use language more precise and definite than the former. There is also another reason for this difference. When a language has no written literature, it is ever subject to a change of pronunciation; and so determinate is the *direction* of these changes, that it may be marked out between limits much narrower than any one has yet ventured to lay down. But with a written literature a new element enters into the calculation. A standard for composition now exists, which the writer will naturally prefer to the varying dialect of the people, and, as far as he safely may, will do his best to follow. In this way the written and the spoken languages will act and react upon each other; and it must depend upon the value of the literature and the reading habits of the people, which of them shall at last prevail. . . The language of our earlier literature fell at last a victim, not to the Norman Conquest, for it survived that event at least a century—not to the foreign jargon which the weak but well-meaning Edward first brought into the country, for French did not *mix* with our language till the days of Chaucer;—it fell before the same deep and mighty influences which swept every living language from the literature of Europe. When the South regained its ascendancy, and Rome once more seized the wealth of vassal provinces, its favourite priests had neither the knowledge requisite to understand, nor tastes fitted to enjoy, the literature of the countries into which they were promoted. The road to their favour and their patronage lay elsewhere ; and the monk giving up his mother tongue as worthless, began to pride himself only upon his Latinity. The legends of his patron saint

he Latinized, the story of his monastery he Latinized; in
Latin he wrote history, in Latin he wrote satires and ro-
mances. Amid these labours he had little time to study
the niceties of Anglo-Saxon grammar; and the Homilies,
the English Scriptures, Caedmon's paraphrase, the national songs, the magnificent Judith, and other treasures
of native genius, must soon have lain on the shelves of his
cloister as little read, or, if read, almost as little understood, as if they had been written in a foreign tongue.
When he addressed himself to the unlearned, noble or
ignoble, he used the vulgar dialect of his shire, with its
idioms, which the written dialect had probably rejected as
wanting in precision, and with its corrupt pronunciation,
which alone would require new forms of grammar. In
this way many specimens of our old English dialects have
been handed down to us; and these, however widely they
differ from each other, agree in one particular,—in con-
founding the characteristic endings of the Anglo-Saxon."

This last statement is explained by a preceding paragraph:—"The Anglo-Saxons had three vowel-endings, *a*,
e, and *u*, to distinguish the cases of the noun and the different conjugations of the verb. In the Old English all
these vowel-endings were represented by the final *e;* and
the loss of the final *e* is the characteristic mark of our
modern dialect. It is obvious that either of these changes
must have brought with it a new language. The confusion of the vowels, or the loss of the final *e*, was a con-
founding of tense and person, of case and number; in
short, of those grammatical forms to which language owes
its precision and its clearness. Other forms were to be
sought for, before our tongue could again serve the purposes of science or of literature."

Mr Guest's solution of the case would, therefore, appear to be, that what brought about the corruption of the

classic Original English (or Saxon) was simply the neglect of that language on the part of the Romish Churchmen, and the preference they were led to give, for literary purposes, to the Latin. But how was it that this cause did not begin to operate till the twelfth century? In England, as elsewhere, Latin had been the professional language of the clergy from the first introduction of Christianity, and had been all along the language in which they usually wrote: witness Beda, Nennius, Asser, and others who lived before the Conquest. Why did not the corruption of the regular into the irregular English, if this was the sole cause of it, take place in the eighth or ninth century?

We venture to think that our recent philology has gone much too far in denying all connexion between the breaking up of the inflectional system of the native language and the Norman Conquest. The view which formerly prevailed was erroneous in regard to the *modus operandi*, or manner in which it was supposed that the effect was produced; it must be admitted that it was not by the Conquest letting in a new language to destroy the purity of the old one by intermixing with it, or to drench it and dissolve its cohesion like an inundation. But that it was really this great political and social revolution which occasioned, though in another way, the extinction, or disuse as a living tongue, of the ancient language of the country in the form in which we have it preserved in the literary works and other writings that have come down to us from the times before the Conquest, seems too evident to admit of being seriously questioned. The facts are only to be explained upon that assumption. There is no similarity between this case and that of the other Germanic and Scandinavian languages which are asserted to have passed

from a highly inflected to a comparatively uninflected
state ; even if it could be admitted to have been clearly
shown that the dissolution or derangement of the original
inflectional structure of the other Low Germanic and
Scandinavian tongues which have been referred to had
been always a purely spontaneous process. The peculi-
arity of the case of the English is, that it had been highly
cultivated and largely employed as a literary language.
It may be safely affirmed that no instance can be produced
of a language so circumstanced which can be shown to
have undergone anything like the same complete and
rapid disintegration or metamorphosis except under the
operation of external causes. Although the principle of
change is continually at work in language, as in everything
else that is not absolutely dead (as if movement and life
were one), its action is always extremely gradual and slow
where it has to contend with the conservative force of a
living literature. The Latin language preserved its grammatical structure in complete integrity so long as it continued to be employed as the literary language of the West ;
the Greek did the same for a thousand years longer,
while it occupied a similar position in the East; and there
seems to be no reason for thinking that either might not
have done so to the present day. It was evidently only
the overthrow of the Western Roman empire and of
western civilisation that occasioned the extinction of the
old grammatical Latin as a living language ; and the
destruction of the Christian civilisation of the East when
Constantinople was conquered and taken possession of by
the Turks that brought the old Greek in like manner to
an end. The stream of the Latin literature, in the one
case, after having flowed on for some eight centuries from
the date of the poets Livius Andronicus and Cneius
Nævius, ceased with Boethius and Cassiodorus; that of

the Greek, in the other, was as suddenly arrested after an existence three times as long. And, in both cases, with the literature the literary language expired. Precisely in the same circumstances and in the same way the old grammatical English appears to have passed out of existence or use. The Conquest of England by the Normans overthrew the peculiar civilisation of which it was at once the creation and the exponent, and the entire social system and condition of things to which it addressed itself and by which it was fed and sustained ; after the Conquest there was no demand for any literature written in the old language, or any public to read it, any more than there remained any public in Italy after the middle of the sixth century sufficiently educated to appreciate works written in good Latin and to stimulate their production, or any educated and wealthy Greek public in Eastern Europe after the conquest of Constantinople by the Turks. In all the three cases we have exactly the same sequence of events, the same chain of causes and consequences :— first, the overthrow of the old social system; next, the cessation of the literature, which was part and parcel of the abolished condition of society and of civilisation ; lastly, the breaking up of the language, which had hitherto been preserved from that fate only by its constant employment in literature. If even so slightly inflected a language as our present English were to cease to be written and to be read, how long would it continue to be correctly spoken ? Hardly for a generation probably.

"The birth of a new language," Mr Bunsen well observes, "presupposes the death of an old one. No language dies without a great crisis occurring in the tribe or nation which speaks it. This crisis may be a great physical revolution, or a voluntary change of country by emigration, or a dissolution of the ancient form of political society by external human force, by invasion, conquest, subjugation. A new language and a new nation are so far identical, that a new language cannot originate without the dissolution of an ancient nationality." (*Christianity and Mankind*, iv. 93).

XIV. In reference to the progress of the vernacular language, the space from about the middle of the Eleventh to the middle of the Thirteenth century, or the first two centuries after the Conquest, has been designated the *Period of Semi-Saxon*. In the popular dialect of this period we have a work of considerable length in verse, the *Chronicle of Layamon*.

LAYAMON'S work has been edited by Sir Frederic Madden, under the title of "Layamon's Brut, or Chronicle of Britain; a poetical Semi-Saxon Paraphrase of the Brut of Wace," with a literal translation, notes, and a glossary, in 3 vols. royal 8vo, London, 1847. Wace was a Norman poet, whose metrical chronicle of Britain, called *Brut d'Angleterre*, was written about the middle of the twelfth century. Layamon, who calls himself a priest of Ernleye upon Severn, that is, of Areley-Regis, near Stourport, in Worcestershire (as first pointed out by Mr Guest in *Penny Cyclopædia*, xx. 488), otherwise called Lower Areley, appears to have written in the latter part of the same century, or in the first half of the second century after the Conquest. Sir Frederic Madden thinks that his work, which extends to above fourteen thousand long verses (divided by Sir Frederic into double that number of hemistichs), was probably completed about A.D. 1200. The views that have been taken of his language, even by the most competent among recent authorities, are not altogether accordant. Mr Price (*Preface to Warton*, 109), commenting upon a remark of Mr Mitford (in his *Harmony of Language*), that it "displays all the appearance of a language thrown into confusion by the circumstances of those who spoke it," affirms that, so far from this being the case, "nearly every important form of Anglo-Saxon grammar is rigidly adhered to; and so little was the language altered at this advanced period of Norman influence, that a few slight alterations might convert it into genuine Anglo-Saxon." Mr Guest (*Eng. Rhythms*, ii. 111, &c.), having observed that one of the most striking peculiarities of Layamon's language is its *nunnation* (from *Nun*, the name of the letter *n* in Hebrew), proceeds:— "Many words end in *n*, which are strangers to that letter, not only in the Anglo-Saxon, but in all the later dialects of our language; and, as this letter assists in the declension of nouns and the conjugation of verbs, the *grammar* of this dialect becomes, to a singular degree, complicated and difficult." Afterwards (p. 186) he says: "Layamon seems to have halted between two languages, the written and the spoken. Now he gives us what appears to be the Old English dialect of the west; and, a few sentences further, we find ourselves entangled in all the peculiarities of the Anglo-Saxon." In the *Penny Cyclopædia* (xx. 488) he remarks that Layamon most probably used the dialect of Worcestershire, the part of the country in which he lived. His English, or Saxon, at any rate, is clearly southern as opposed to northern, and western as opposed to eastern.

Sir Frederic Madden (*Pref. xxv.*) also holds that the dialect of Layamon's poem must be taken to be that of North Worcestershire, the district in which the writer lived. Although this locality was within the bounds of what was called the kingdom of Mercia, the dialect, he

observes, is decidedly that of the west, which was substantially the same with that of the south, of England.
He thinks there can be no doubt that the written language of the country, previous to the Conquest, was
more stable in its character and more observant of grammatical accuracy than the spoken; and that there are
many reasons to induce us to believe that the spoken
language in the reign of Edward the Confessor did not
materially differ from that which is found in manuscripts
a century later (*Pref.* xxvii.). " The language of Layamon," he then goes on, " belongs to that transition period
in which the groundwork of Anglo-Saxon phraseology
and grammar still existed, although gradually yielding
to the influence of the popular forms of speech. We
find in it, as in the later portion of the *Saxon Chronicle,*
marked indications of a tendency to adopt those terminations and sounds which characterise a language in a state
of change, and which are apparent also in some other
branches of the Teutonic tongue." The peculiarities
distinguishing it from the pure Anglo-Saxon he enumerates as being :—" The use of *a* as an article ;—the change
of the Anglo-Saxon, or classic English of the earliest form,
terminations *a* and *an* into *e* and *en*, as well as the disre-
gard of inflections and genders ;—the masculine forms
given to neuter nouns in the plural ;—the neglect of the
feminine terminations of adjectives and pronouns, and
confusion between the definite and indefinite declensions ;
—the introduction of the preposition *to* before infinitives,
and occasional use of weak tenses of verbs and participles
instead of strong ;—the constant occurrence of *en* for *on*
in the plurals of verbs, and frequent elision of the final
e ;—together with the uncertainty of the rule for the
government of prepositions." There are also, it is added,

F

numerous vowel-changes, which, however, are not altogether arbitrary.

The *nunnation* in which Layamon indulges, or his "addition of a final *n* to certain cases of nouns and adjectives, to some tenses of verbs, and to several other parts of speech," is characterised by his editor as being by no means uniform or constant, and as in numerous instances of final rhyme possibly used only for the sake of euphony, that is, of supplying the requisite consonance. Its use, Sir Frederic thinks, was probably restricted to the dialect in which the poem is written. We have the poem in two texts, both apparently of the thirteenth century, but one probably a little later than the other. There is less of nunnation in the later text. And even in the earlier, we are told, "there are many passages in which it has been struck out or erased by a second hand, and sometimes by the first; so that it is manifest that some doubt must have existed as to the propriety of its usage."

The distinguishing marks of the western dialect in Layamon are enumerated by Sir Frederic as being chiefly "the termination of the present tense plural in *th*, and infinitives in *i*, *ie*, or *y*; the forms of the plural personal pronouns, *heo*, *heore*, *heom*; the frequent occurrence of the prefix *i* before past participles; the use of *v* for *f*, and prevalence of the vowel *u* for *i* or *y*, in such words as *dude*, *hudde*, *hulle*, *putte*, *hure*, &c." In the later text he conceives an Anglian or northern element to have probably been infused into the dialect. This text he thinks may perhaps have been written on the east side of Leicestershire.

"The structure of Layamon's poem," says Sir Frederic, "consists partly of lines in which the alliterative system of the Anglo-Saxons is preserved, and partly of couplets of unequal length rhiming together. Many couplets, indeed, occur which have both of these forms, whilst others are often met with which possess neither. The latter therefore must have depended wholly on accentuation, or have been corrupted in transcription. The relative proportion of each of these forms is not to be ascertained without extreme difficulty, since the author uses them everywhere intermixed, and slides from alliteration to rhime, or from rhime to alliteration, in a manner perfectly arbitrary. The alliterative portion, however, predominates on the whole greatly over the lines rhiming together, even including the imperfect or assonant terminations, which are very frequent." And he refers to the fullest and most learned discussion which the subject has received, that by Mr Guest, who, in his *History of English Rhythms*, II. 114—124, gives a long specimen of the poem with the accents marked, both of the alliterative and rhiming couplets, and shows that the latter "are founded on the models of accentuated Anglo-Saxon rhythms of four, five, six, or seven accents," those of six and of five accents being used most frequently.*

---

* "An Anglo-Saxon verse," says Mr Guest (Pen. Cycl. xx. 489, art. *Saxon Language and Literature*), "is made up of two sections, which together may contain four, five, six, or even more accented syllables. These sections are bound together by the law of alliteration, or, in other words, each verse must have at least two accented syllables (one in each section) beginning with the same consonant or with vowels." But he adds.—"It is very incorrect to call this alliteration the 'essence' or the 'groundwork' of Anglo-Saxon verse. It is certainly an important part, but still a mere adjunct. The purposes it served were similar to those which are provided for by the final rhyme of our modern versification. The essence of Anglo-Saxon verse consisted in its system of rhythm."

XV. After the middle of the Thirteenth century, the
language assumes the general shape and physiognomy of the English which we now write and
speak. It may be called English rough-hewn.
The space from about the middle of the Thirteenth
to the middle of the Fourteenth century has been
usually designated the *Period of Old or* (better)
Early English.

ANOTHER work in verse is commonly mentioned along
with *Layamon's Chronicle* as of the same age; that
known as the *Ormulum,* from its author, who calls himself *Ormin* or *Orm.* Considerable extracts from the
Ormulum had been given by Hickes and Wanley, and
in Mr Guest's and other modern works; but the whole
has now been printed.* Hickes goes so far as to
place it among the first writings after the Conquest.
Tyrwhitt, who, in his *Essay on the Language and Versification of Chaucer,* was the first to point out that it was
written in verse, only ventures to say that he cannot
conceive it to be of earlier date than the reign of Henry
the Second (or the latter half of the twelfth century).
Mr Guest, who, although he seems in one place (*Eng.
Rhythms,* i. 107) to speak of Ormin as having written
in the beginning of the thirteenth century, elsewhere (ii.

---

* "Edited from the original Manuscript in the Bodleian, with
Notes and a Glossary, by Robert Meadows White, D.D., formerly
Professor of Anglo-Saxon in the University of Oxford;" 2 vols. 8vo,
Oxford, 1852. (At the University Press.)

185) assigns his poem to the latter half of the twelfth, considers it "the oldest, the purest, and by far the most valuable specimen of our Old English dialect that time has left us." He adds:—"Ormin used the dialect of his day; and, when he wanted precision or uniformity, he followed out the principles on which that dialect rested. Were we thoroughly masters of his grammar and vocabulary, we might hope to explain many of the difficulties in which blunders of transcription and a transitional state of the language have involved the syntax and the prosody of Chaucer." (*Ibid.*) Afterwards (ii. 209), he intimates that, if he were called upon to say in what part of England a dialect such as Ormin's was ever spoken, he would fix upon some county north of Thames and south of Lincolnshire.

The *Ormulum* consists of a series of metrical homilies and passages from Scripture read in the service of the Church. What we have appears to be only a portion of the work; but it extends to about 20,000 lines, two of which, however, may be considered as making only one line in another kind of measure. Ormin has given a remarkable appearance to his language by a spelling peculiar to himself, which seems to consist in always doubling the consonant after a vowel having any other than the sound that would be given to it by a single consonant followed by a silent *e*. He attaches great importance to this device, expressly charging all who may copy his book to write the letters twice wherever he has himself done so, and assuring them that otherwise they will not write the word aright. The effect will be seen in the following short specimen:—

"Godd seggde thuss till Abraham; Tacc Ysaac thin wennchell,
And snith itt, alls itt wære an shep, And legg itt upponn allterr,
And brenn itt all till asskess thær, And offre itt me to lake.

And Abraham wass forrthrihht bun To don Drihhtiness wille,
And toc hiss sune sone anan, And band itt fët and hande,
And leggde itt upponn allterr swa, And droh hiss swerd off shœthe,
And hof the swerd upp withth hiss hannd To smitenn itt to dœde;
Forr thatt he wollde ben till Godd Herrsumm onn alle wise.
And Godd sahh thatt he wollde slaen The child withth swerdess
    egge,
And seggde thuss till Habraham, Thatt witt tu wel to sothe,
Hald, Abraham, hald upp thin hannd, Ne sla thu nohht tin wenn-
    chell;
Nu wät I thatt tu drædesst Godd, And lufesst Godd withth herrte ;
Tacc thær an shep bafftenn thin bacc, And offre itt forr the wennchell.
And Abraham tha snath thatt shep, And lett hiss sune libbenn ;
Forr thatt he wollde ben till Godd Hersumm onn alle wise."

                            v. 14,664—14,693.

That is, in our present English :—

God said thus to Abraham :—Take Isaac, thine child,
And slay it as it were an sheep, and lay it upon [the] altar,
And burn it all to ashes there, and offer it me for gift.
And Abraham was forthwith bound [engaged in proceeding] to do
    [the] Lord's will,
And took his son soon anon, and bound him foot and hand,*
And laid it upon [the] altar so, and drew his sword [out] of sheath,
And heaved the sword up with his hand to smite it to death ;
For that he would be to God obedient in all wise.
And God saw that he would [was willing to] slay the child with
    sword's edge,
And said thus to Abraham (that wot thou well for sooth) ;
Hold, Abraham, hold up thine hand, nor slay thou not thine
    child ;
Now know I that thou dreadest God, and lovest God with heart,
Take there an sheep behind thine back, and offer it for the
    child.
And Abraham then slew the sheep, and let his son live ;
For that he would be to God obedient in all wise.

---

* Mr Guest translates " fect and hands," understanding the *e* in
hande to be the sign of the plural.   See *post*, under Sect. xix.

It is impossible to compare *Layamon* and the *Ormulum* without being led to entertain the strongest doubts as to the correctness of the common assumption that they are works of the same age. They do not exhibit the language in the same stage, or, at least, in the same state. The grammar of *Layamon* is half, or more than half, that of Original English, or the English of the time before the Conquest; it may be questioned if that of the *Ormulum* have retained a vestige of what is peculiar to that form of the language. If it were certain that the two works were contemporary, we should be compelled to conclude that the people of the west were still speaking English of the first form while those of the eastern counties were speaking English of the second form. But, in truth, there is no evidence that the *Ormulum* is as old as *Layamon*. Like many other pieces which have been assigned to the twelfth century, the *Ormulum* is much more probably of the latter part of the thirteenth.* In that case, *Layamon* and it will belong, according to the arrangement here adopted, to different periods in the history of the language. (*Vid.* Sect. xx.)

Ormin's peculiar spelling may probably have preserved something of the history of the language. If it was his

---

* "It may be proper to observe here," says Price, in a note on the First Section of Warton's *History*,—in which several of these pieces are brought forward, although the *Ormulum* is not mentioned,—" that the dates assigned to the several compositions quoted in this Section are extremely arbitrary and uncertain. Judging from internal evidence—a far more satisfactory criterion than Warton's computed age of his MSS.—there is not one which may not safely be referred to the thirteenth century, and by far the greater number to the close of that period." Many important additional remarks upon these compositions will be found in the Notes to the Second Edition of *Price's Warton* (3 vols. 8vo, 1840), vol. i. pp. 1—42.

rule always to leave the consonant single after the long or *name* sound (as in *mate, meet, mite, mote, mute*), and to double it after every vowel otherwise sounded, then from the short passage which has been quoted above we should learn that, while *God, thus, till, up, will, his, off, wit, for, edge, back, it, his, with, on, that*, were all pronounced in his day, as at present, with the *shut* sound, *thine, sheep, smite* (or *smiten*), *child*, took, as they now do, the *name* sound; that the *e* in *legg* (*lay*) and in the first syllable of *seggde* (*said*) was sounded as in our *egg;* that *snith* and *snath* rhymed not to our *lith* and *lath*, but to our *lithe* and *lathe;* that *bun* was probably pronounced *boon*, and *don, doon* or *dun;* that *toc* was called *took*, and the first syllable of *sothe, sooth*, as at present; that *hof* was probably sounded *hofe*, or *hove;* that they probably said, not *luffest* or *lovest* (as we do), but *loofest* or *loovest;* that *an* was sounded *ain* (as in *lane*); that *heart* was called *hert* (not *heert*); and that, on the other hand, the word for a *sword* was pronounced not *swerd*, but *sweerd*. *And*, however, which is usually indicated in the MS. by a contraction, was probably pronounced as at present.

What is commonly given as our earliest specimen of *English* (as distinguished from what is called *Semi-Saxon*) is a proclamation issued in 1258, in the name of King Henry III., while under the control of the Council appointed at what is called "the mad parliament" of Oxford, of which the following is the copy addressed to the people of Huntingdonshire :—

"Henr' thurg godes fultume King on Engleneloande Lhoauerd on Yrloand Duk on Norm' on Aquitain' and Eorl on Aniow, send igretinge to alle hise halde, ilaerde and ilaewed, on Huntendon' schir'

"Thaet witen ge wel alle thaet we willen and vnnen thaet, thaet ure raedesmen alle other the moare dael of heom thaet beoth ichosen thurg us and thurg thaet loandes folk one vre kuneriche habbeth idon and schullen don in the worthnesse of gode, and on vre treowthe for the freme of the loande thurg the besigte of than to foreniseide redesmen beo stedefaest and ilestinde in alle thinge abuten aende

"And we hoaten alle vre treowe in the treowthe thaet heo vs ogen thaet heo stedefaesliche healden and swerien to healden and to werien the isetnesses thet beon imakede and beon to makien thurg than to foren iseide raedesmen other thurg the moare dael of heom alswo alse hit is biforen iseid.

"And thaet aehc other helpe thaet for to done bi than ilche othe agenes alle men rigt for to done and to foangen. and non ne mine of loand ne of egtewherthurg this besigte muge beon ilet other iwersed on onie wise. And gif oni other onie cumen her ongenes we willen and hoaten thaet alle vre treowe heom healden deadlicheistan.

"And for thaet we willen thaet this beo stedefaest and lestinde We senden gew this writ open iseined with vre seel to halden amanges gew ine hord. Witnesse usselvien aet Lunden', thane egtetenthe day on the monthe of Octobr' in the two and fowertighte yeare of vre cruninge."

Henry, through God's help, King in England, Lord in Ireland, Duke in Normandy, in Aquitain, and Earl in Anjou, sends greeting to all his subjects, learned and lay, in Huntingdonshire.

This know ye well all that we will and grant that that our counsellors, all or the more part of them, that be chosen through us and through the land's folk in our kingdom, have done and shall do, in the honour of God and in our truth [allegiance], for the good of the land, through the business [act] of those to-foresaid counsellors, be steadfast and lasting in all things but [without] end.

And we enjoin all our lieges, in the truth [allegiance] that they us owe, that they steadfastly hold, and swear to hold and to defend, the ordinances that be made and be to make through the to-foresaid counsellors, or through the more part of them, all so as it is before said.

And that each other help that for to do, by them [to] each other against all men right for to do and to promote. And none, nor of my land nor elsewhere, through this business may be let [hindered] or damaged in any wise. And if any man or any woman come them against, we will and enjoin that all our lieges them hold deadly foes.

And, for that we will that this be steadfast and lasting, we send you this writ open, signed with our seal, to hold amongst you in hoard [store]. Witness ourselves at London, this eighteenth day in the month of October, in the two and fortieth year of our crowning.*

But this official paper can scarcely be safely quoted as exhibiting the current language of the time. Like all such documents, it is made up in great part of established phrases of form, many of which had probably become obsolete in ordinary speech and writing. The English of the proclamation of 1258 is much less modern than that of the *Ormulum*, and fully as near to the earlier form of

---

* This proclamation was first printed by Somner, in his *Dictionarium Saxonico-Latino-Anglicum*, fol. Oxon. 1659. In the Record Commission edition of *Rymer's Fœdera*, vol. i. (1816), p. 378, it is entitled, " Carta Regis in idiomate Anglico, ad singulos comitatus Angliæ et Hiberniæ super reformatione statûs regni per proceres ejusdem regni ; " and'is stated to be there given as transcribed from the original among the Patent Rolls in the Tower of London (" Pat. 43, Hen. III. m. 15, in Turr. Lond."). The present transcript, however, will be found, we believe, to be more correct than any hitherto published.

" This proclamation," Dr Lingard observes, " is in both languages [English and French], the first of that description which has been preserved since the reign of Henry I., though I do not understand how such proclamations could have become known to the people unless they were published in the English language." *Hist. Eng.* III. 125.

the language, both in the words and in the grammar, as any part of *Layamon's Chronicle*, if not rather more so.

Exclusive of the *Ormulum*, the two principal literary works belonging to this period, 1250—1350 (commonly known as that of *Early English*), are the metrical Chronicles of *Robert of Gloucester* and *Robert of Brunne*.

The Chronicle of Robert of Gloucester was edited by Thomas Hearne in 1724. The writer may be regarded as belonging to the first half of the present period: it has been shown by Sir Frederic Madden (*Introd. to Havelok, lii.*) that he must have survived the year 1297. The following passage is doubly curious in reference to the history of the language :—

> "Thus come lo ! Engelond into Normannes honde,
> And the Normans ne couthe speke tho bote her owe speche,
> And speke French as dude atom, and here chyldren dude al so teche ;
> So that heymen of thys lond, that of her blod come,
> Holdeth alle thulke speche that hii of hem nome ;
> Vor bote a man couthe French me tolth of hym wel lute :
> Ac lowe men holdeth to Englyss and to her kunde speche yute.
> Ich wene ther ne be man in world contreyes none
> That ne holdeth to her kunde speche, bote Engelond one.
> Ac wel me wot vor to conne both wel yt ys ;
> Vor the more that a man con, the more worth he ys." *

That is, in modern words :—Thus came lo ! England into Normans' hand. And the Normans no could speak then but their own speech, and spake French as [they] did at home, and their children did all so teach ; so that high-men of this land, that of their blood come, hold all the same speech that they of them took ; for but a man know French one [*homme*, or *on*] telleth [reckoneth] of

---

* *Hearne*, 364 ; *Harl. MS.* 201, *fol.* 127, r°.

him well little [*bien peu*] : but low men hold to English
and to their natural speech yet. I ween there no be man
in world countries none that no holdeth to their natural
speech, but England [al-]one. But well I wot for to
know both well it is; for the more that a man know, the
more worth he is.

Some of the peculiarities in the language of Robert of
Gloucester are probably to be attributed to the dialect he
uses being that of the west of England. *Robert of Brunne*,
that is, *Bourne*, in Lincolnshire, may be assumed to have
written in that of the east country. His proper name
appears to have been Robert Manning ; and he may be
placed nearly half a century later than Robert of Gloucester. His *Chronicle* is stated to have been finished in the
year 1338. It consists of two parts; the first of which
is in octo-syllabic rhyme, and is a translation from Wace's
Brut, the same original upon which Layamon worked;
the second is in Alexandrine verse, and is translated from
a French chronicle recently written by an Englishman,
Piers or Peter de Langtoft, a canon regular of St. Austin,
at Bridlington in Yorkshire. Only the second part has
been printed : it was edited by Hearne in 1725.

Robert de Brunne distinctly claims to be considered
as writing in *English ;* and he is said to be the earliest
writer after the Conquest who uniformly and pointedly
gives that name to his language.

The following passages are from the Prologue to the
First Part of the *Chronicle*, which Hearne has printed in
the Preface to his edition of the Second Part :—

" Lordynges [*Lords*] that be now here,
   If ye wille listene and lere [*learn*]
   All the story of Inglande,
   Als [*as*] Robert Mannyng wryten it fand [*written it found*],

And on [*in*] Inglysch has it schewed,
Not for the lered [*learned*], bot for the lewed [*unlearned*];
For tho [*those*] that on this lond wonn [*dwell*]
That the Latin ne Frankys conn [*Latin nor French know*],
˙For to haf solace and gamen [*game, enjoyment*]
In felauschip when thai [*they*] sitt samen [*together*].

     .   .   .   .   .   .

After the Bretons the Inglis camen;
The lordschip of this lande thai namen [*took*];
South and north, west and est,
That calle men now the Inglis gest [*history ?*]
When thai first among the Bretons,
That now ere [*are*] Inglis, than [*then*] were Saxons,
Saxons, Inglis, hight alle oliche [*were called all alike*].

     .   .   .   .   .   .

I mad noght for no disours [*diseurs, professed tale-tellers*],
Ne [*nor*] for no seggers [*sayers, reciters*] no [*nor*] harpours,
But for the luf [*love*] of symple men,
That strange Inglis can not ken [*know, understand*];
For many it ere [*there are*] that strange Inglis
In ryme wate [*wot, know*] neuer what it is.

     .   .   .   .   .   .

Of Brunne I am, if any me blame;
Robert Mannyng is my name:
Blissed be he of God of heuene [*heaven*],
That me Robert with gude wille neuene [*named*].
In the thrid Edwarde's tyme was I
When I wrote alle this story.
In the hous of Sixille I was a throwe [*while*];
Dans [*Dominus*] Robert of Maltone, that ye know
Did [*caused*] it write for felawes [*brother monks'*] sake,
When thai wild solace make."

XVI. Meanwhile, in the literature of the country, and
also in the oral intercourse of the most influential
classes of the population, the native language may
be said to have been for the First century after the
Norman Conquest completely overborne by the
French; for the Second, to have been in a state of
revolt against that foreign tongue; during the
Third, to have been rapidly making head against
the intruder, and regaining its old supremacy.

Or the three stages may be thus distinguished :—The
first, comprehending the reigns of the Conqueror, his two
sons, and Stephen, a space of 88 years; the second, the
reigns of Henry II., his two sons, and Henry III., a space
of 118 years; the third, the reigns of Edward I., II., and
III., a space of 105 years.*   In a loose or general way the
first and second of these spaces will correspond to what
has been designated the Period of Semi-Saxon, the third
to what is commonly called the Period of Early English.

What professes to be our earliest notice of the introduction of the French tongue into England, and of the
extent to which it speedily came to be used, is found in

* The reign of *William I.* (*the Conqueror*) began in 1066 ; that of
his son, *William II.* (*Rufus*), in 1087 ; that of his brother, *Henry I.*,
in 1100 ; that of *Stephen* in 1135; that of *Henry II.* in 1154; that
of his son, *Richard I.* (*Cœur de Lion*), in 1189; that of his brother,
John, in 1199; that of his son, *Henry III.*, in 1216; that of his son,
Edward I., in 1272 ; that of his son, *Edward II.*, in 1307; that of his
son, *Edward III.*, in 1327; and he reigned till 1377, or 311 years from
the Conquest.

the work styled the History of the Abbey of Croyland by Ingulphus (*Ingulfi Croylandensis Historia*). Ingulphus was abbot of the monastery of Croyland, or Crowland, in Lincolnshire, from A.D. 1075 till 1109, when he died at the age of eighty. He was, therefore, at the time of the Norman Conquest, a man of between thirty and forty. But the *History* which bears his name is now generally regarded as being in the main a forgery of a later age, most probably of the beginning of the fourteenth or the end of the thirteenth century. It may, however, have been founded in part upon traditions or even documents of earlier origin. The amount of what it states upon the present subject is :—That even before the Conquest, in the reign of the Confessor, all the English nobility, following the fashion of the king, himself a Norman in all his habits and feelings, and of the other Normans with whom he had filled the highest offices in the kingdom, began both to speak French and to have their charters and other writings drawn up in that language ; and that, after the Conquest, not only were the laws and statutes of the realm promulgated in French, but that language was substituted for English in teaching boys at school the elements of grammar. The fact, however, is, as has been already stated, that the laws were published in Latin for more than two centuries after the Conquest. If they were ever also published in French, which is doubtful, and can hardly have been the case except in a few instances, the French was apparently a translation from the Latin.*

* This, at any rate, was probably the case with what are called the Laws of the Conqueror, which are given by Ingulphus in French (See Sir Francis Palgrave's *Rise and Progress of the English Commonwealth*, pp. 55 *et seq.*, and his *Proofs and Illustrations*, pp. *lxxxviii—civ.*, containing the Latin text, published for the first time from the *Holkham*

Warton and Tyrwhitt have collected various testimonies which amply confirm what is stated in the Croyland History as to the employment of French in the education of youth, and the general prevalence of that language in England for a long time after the Conquest. It is mentioned by Gervase of Tilbury, a writer of the early part of the thirteenth century, that in his time the English nobility always sent their children to be brought up in France. The statements of Robert of Gloucester at the close of that century, and of Robert Holcot in the beginning and Ralph Higden about the middle of the next, have been already referred to (*Vid.* pp. 48 and 75).

It is also known, not only from the recorded names and accounts of the writers, but from many remains that have come down to us, that an abundant production of literature in the French language was carried on both by foreigners resident at the English court and by Englishmen for some centuries after the Conquest. In all light or popular literature French was at first the only language employed ; it continued to predominate for some time after the English had begun to come into use ; nor, even after the latter had acquired the ascendancy, did its foreign rival cease to be occasionally resorted to. It is evident that French must have been more familiar than English to a considerable section of the inhabitants of England down to the end of the fourteenth century.*

MS.). An opposite view, however, has been taken by Luders (*Tracts, pp.* 392, 393) of the French text of Magna Charta, first published in D'Achery's *Spicilegium,* which he regards as the original.

* See, however, what has been advanced by Mr Guest in opposition to or in qualification of this view, in his *History of English Rhythms,* ii. 427. He conceives that the French, or Romance language as it was called, was in the twelfth and thirteenth centuries "a dead language, learnt only from books ; " and, while he allows that it "must have been

The declension and extinction of the French language in England were probably precipitated by the strong anti-Gallican feeling engendered by the French wars of Edward III., which began a few years before the middle of the fourteenth century.

The discontinuance of French as the medium for the instruction of boys in Latin is expressly noted by John de Trevisa, in a paragraph which he inserts in his translation of Higden's Chronicle after the passage recording the fact of the previous usage, to have taken place about that date, or, as he puts it, immediately after the first great plague, which was in the year 1349. The authors of the innovation, he says, were a grammar school-master, named John Cornwall, and his pupil, Richard Pencrich. Trevisa writes this account in the year 1385.*

Meanwhile, in 1362, the 36th year of Edward III., it was ordered by act of parliament that all trials at law should henceforth be conducted in English. In the preamble of the act it is averred that the French tongue, in which pleas had heretofore been pleaded, was become much unknown in the realm, so that the people who impleaded or were impleaded in the king's and other courts had no knowledge nor understanding of what was said for them or against them by their sergeants and other pleaders.

more or less familiar to the scholar as well as to the courtier," he holds it to be clear that " it did not reach to the great body of the people," from "the many versions of Romance poems made *for the lewed man*," a phrase which, he observes, includes both *lord* and yeoman. But how are we to account for the existence of the Romance originals of those versions, and of a large body of Romance literature besides, which we have no reason to believe ever was translated, except upon the supposition that the French language was more familiar than the English to a large portion of the English reading public?

* See it in Appendix.

G

Yet this very statute is in French, as all statutes continued to be for more than a century longer. The first in English is in the 1st year of Henry VII. (1485); and even that is also in French. It is only from 1488-9, the 4th of Henry VII., that English alone is used. The proceedings of the House of Lords were recorded in French down to a still later date. Certain parliamentary forms, indeed, are still in that language. French also continued to be the language in which the published reports of law cases were usually drawn up till the middle of the seventeenth century; nor did its employment for that purpose altogether cease till some time after the commencement of the eighteenth.

By the statute of 1362 pleas were ordered to be always entered and enrolled in Latin (instead of sometimes in Latin, sometimes in French, as had been heretofore the practice). This would seem to show that the statute was instigated more by spite against the French language than by affection for the English.

XVII. In the course of the contest between the two languages the English had undergone a considerable alteration of its vocabulary by the reception of words from the French, many of which had probably displaced or rendered obsolete equivalent terms of native origin; so that, by the time it had come to be fully established and recognised, in the latter part of the fourteenth century, as the proper literary language of the country, it had been transformed from a purely Gothic into a partially Neo-Latin language.

THE French language in England was only an exotic, which, introduced by force, was for a time sustained, and even disseminated within certain limits, by the same force which had imported it, but could not, in the nature of things, continue to maintain an independent existence in the country after the originally foreign domination with which it was brought in had come to be completely nationalised.

Yet in the same manner, and, perhaps, nearly in the same degree, in which the old political constitution of the country has been permanently modified by that which the Normans established in its stead, has the old language been affected and changed by intermixture with that of the Normans.

It may be held to be now admitted on all hands that it is only in the vocabulary of the English language that any intrusion or direct action of the French is to be traced. Such change as the grammar has undergone certainly has not been produced by the adoption of any part of the grammar of its rival.

There has been considerable difference of opinion, however, in regard to the date at which the partial transformation of the vocabulary of the English by absorption from the French began to show itself. Tyrwhitt refers to the writings both of Robert of Brunne and Robert of Gloucester as evidencing that this process had fairly commenced in the thirteenth century; Mr Guest, nevertheless, as we have seen (see *ante*, p. 57), has intimated his adherence to the old opinion, that " French did not mix with our language till the days of Chaucer," or till nearly a century after the time of Robert of Gloucester.

Tyrwhitt asks if it be credible that "a poet writing in English [as was Chaucer's case] upon the most familiar subjects would stuff his compositions with French words and phrases," if such words and phrases had not been generally intelligible to his readers, that is to say, if they had not already taken their place in the common or national language? " Or," it is added, "if he had been so very absurd, is it conceivable that he should have immediately become, not only the most admired, but also the most popular, writer of his time and country?"

Chaucer has nowhere evinced any special partiality for the French language. He derides (in his description of the Prioress in the *Prologue* to the *Canterbury Tales*) the French spoken in England; and in his prose tract entitled *The Testament of Love* he speaks with contempt of such of his countrymen as still continued to "speke their poysy mater" in that foreign tongue; adding, " Let, then, clerkes endyten in Latyn, for they have the propertye in science and the knowinge in that facultye, and lette Frenchmen in their Frenche also endyte their queynt termes, for it is kyndly [*natural*] to theyr mouthes ; and let us shewe our fantasyes in such wordes as we learneden of our dames tonge,"—that is, what we now call our mother tongue, the tongue we learn from our mothers.

The proportion of words of French derivation in the English, not only of Chaucer, but of the generality of Chaucer's contemporaries, in that, for instance, of Mandevil and Wiclif, is far too large to be accounted for except on the hypothesis that the vocabulary of the one language had then been flowing into the other for a considerable time.

It is probable that this process had been going on almost from the birth of the new form of the English language and of English literature, as distinguished from what have been called Saxon and Semi-Saxon, that is to say, from the middle of the thirteenth century. It was the natural consequence of the relative position of the two languages and the two literatures,—the one (the English) mainly the offspring and imitator of the other (the French), and seeking to make itself acceptable to the same community the most influential portion of which had so long patronised its predecessor.

The English language, probably, would not have acquired the ascendancy so soon as it did if it had not thus assumed a partially French guise or character, and so enabled itself the more easily to become a substitute for French, and to win its way with the most cultivated class of readers.

It was, no doubt, principally through the medium of literary compositions that French words were at first introduced into the English language. Many of the earliest works written in English were translations, more or less free, from the French ; and the translator would in many cases have every temptation to retain an expressive term in his original, rather than to beat his brains in attempting to find or to fabricate a vernacular equivalent. A French word introduced now and then would be an impediment to no reader, and would by many or most be regarded as rather ornamental.

At the same time the intrusion of words formed from the French was, probably, facilitated by the broken down or uncemented condition of the English language at this date, which disabled it from producing new terms, when wanted, out of his own resources as readily as the primitive form of the language, with its more inflectional structure, might have done.

The total, or all but total, absence of Latin in the Original English (with the exception only of the theological and learned words for which it was indebted to the Roman ecclesiastics) is a remarkable fact, and one of great importance; but rather in reference to the history of the country than to that of the language. It is somewhat strange that few or none even of the words which the Gothic conquerors of Britain are supposed to have adopted from the Welsh language appear to be of Latin original.

XVIII. Our modern standard English, in so far as it is of native origin, appears to have grown out of a dialect formed in the Midland Counties by such an intermixture of the Northern and Southern dialects as rejected the more remarkable peculiarities of both.

THE question of the local origin of standard English forms the subject of an interesting disquisition by Mr Guest, which will be found in the *History of English Rhythms*, ii. 187—207.

Mr Guest's view is founded in part upon a passage (already referred to) in the Latin Chronicle of Ralph Higden, written about or shortly before the middle of the fourteenth century, in which, after stating that the English had originally among them three different dialects,—southern, midland, and northern,—but that, having become mixed first with Danes, and afterwards with Normans, they had in many respects corrupted their own tongue, and now affected a sort of outlandish babble, Higden goes on :—" In the above threefold Saxon tongue, which has barely survived among a few country people, the men of the east agree more in speech with those of the west—as being situated under the same quarter of the heavens—than the northern men with the southern. Hence it is that the Mercians,* or midland English—

---

* The name of *Mercia*, or the *March*, was given to that one of the Anglo-Saxon kingdoms which bordered on the Welsh territory, and which in its greatest extent came to include all the middle of England, or (with the exception of Wales in the west and East Anglia in the east) the whole range of country between the Trent and the Ribble in the north, and the Thames and the Bristol Avon in the south.

partaking, as it were, the nature of the extremes—understand the adjoining dialects, the northern and the southern, better than those last understand each other. The whole speech of the Northumbrians, especially in Yorkshire, is so harsh and rude, that we southern men can hardly understand it.''

The country of the northern dialect, or dialects, Mr Guest extends as far south as to the Thames. That the dialects spoken to the north of that river possessed a common character, which long distinguished them from the southern dialects, he thinks may be shown even at the present day. The inflections of the northern verb, in particular, differ from those of the southern :—The pres. ind. was, in the southern, *Ich hop-e, Thou hop-est, He hop-eth, We, Ye, Hi hop-eth;* in the northern, *I hop-es, Thou hop-es, He hop-es, We, Ye, Hi hop-es :* the second per. sing. perf. ind. was, in the southern, *Thou hoped-est ;* in the northern, *Thou hoped-es :* the second per. sing. pres. imper. was, in the southern, *Hop-eth ye ;* in the northern, *Hop-es ye :* the pres. infin. was, in the southern, *To hop-en ;* in the northern, *To hope.* In the northern inflections, Mr Guest holds, we may detect those of a conjugation which is fully developed in the Swedish. Then, after noticing other peculiarities, he proceeds ;—'' It is a curious fact that both our universities are situated close to the boundary line which separated the northern from the southern English : and I cannot help thinking, that the jealousies of these two races were consulted in fixing upon the sites. The histories of Cambridge and Oxford are filled with their feuds ; and more than once has the king's authority been interposed, to prevent the northern men retiring, and forming within their own limits a university at Stamford or Northampton. The union of these two races at the university must have favoured the growth of any intermediate dialect; and to such a dialect the circumstances of the country, during the ninth and tenth centuries, appear to have given birth. While the north was sinking beneath its own feuds and the ravages of the Northman, the closest ties knit together the men of the midland and the southern counties; and this fellowship seems to have led, among the former, to a certain modification of the northern dialect. The change seems to have been brought about, not so much by adopting the peculiarities of southern speech, as by giving greater prominence to such parts of the native dialect as were common to the south. The southern conjugations must, at all times, have been familiar (at least in dignified composition) to the natives of the northern counties, but other conjugations were *popularly* used, and in the gradual disuse of these, and other forms peculiar to the north, the change consisted."

By these and other reasons Mr Guest is led to the conclusion "that in the middle of the fourteenth century there were *three* great English dialects—the northern, the midland, and the southern;" and he thinks, "that, even amid the multiplied varieties of the present day, these three divisions may yet be traced." Two vigorous efforts, he adds, were made to detain and preserve the northern dialect as it was retreating northwards, and to fix it as a literary language: the first, in the thirteenth century, by the men of Lincolnshire; the second, in the fifteenth century, by the men of Lothian; "but the convenience of a dialect essentially the same as the northern, and far more widely understood, its literary wealth, and latterly the patronage of the court, gave the midland English an ascendancy that gradually swept all rivalry before it." The southern dialect, however, kept its ground more firmly than the northern; little more than.

two centuries having gone by since it first began to give way before the midland dialect.

Mr Guest divides the midland dialect into *six* varieties; and one of them, which he would term the Leicestershire dialect, and which is described as "remarkable for its want of tone," has, he conceives, "contributed, more than any of our [other] living dialects, to the formation of our present standard English."

Dr Latham (*English Language*, 555), holding that the parts where the purest English is most generally spoken are those between Huntingdon and Stamford, and agreeing with Mr Guest so far as to think it nearly certain " that the dialect most closely allied to the dialect (or dialects) out of which the present literary language of England is developed is to be found either in Northamptonshire or the neighbouring counties," is inclined to look for it, not with Mr Guest, in Leicestershire, on the western side of that county, but rather in Huntingdonshire, on the eastern side.

XIX. The space from about the middle of the Fourteenth to the middle of the Sixteenth Century has been styled the *Period of Middle English;* and that designation may be understood to express not only the position of the Period, but the fact that the existing modification of the language, in respect both of its vocabulary and of its grammar, was then in a state of transition from its earliest and rudest form to that in which it was ultimately to rest. To the commencement of this Period belong the writings of Chaucer, the Homer of our Poetry and the true Father of English Literature.

As has been pointed out by Mr Guest (*Eng. Rhythms,* ii. 105), the characteristic distinction of Old (or Early) English, as compared with the original form of the language, is the employment of the one termination *e,* in the declension of nouns and the conjugation of verbs, to represent indiscriminately the three ancient vowel-endings, *a, e,* and *u.* In this way the ancient *nama, ende,* and *wudu* became in Early English *nam-e, end-e,* and *wood-e,* or *wood-de.* Now the distinction of Middle English, as compared with Early English, may be defined as being the tendency to drop this final *e* as a distinct syllable, and, along with that simplification, to throw off also whatever else remained of the original inflectional system of the language.

Chaucer is believed to have died, at the age of seventy-two, in the year 1400. His writings may, therefore, be received as exemplifying the state of the language in the first half century of the present period.

Even if we had no positive evidence on the subject, it would be impossible to believe that the language of a great popular poet could be other than substantially the language of his own age,—written, perhaps, with more regularity and refinement by him than by others, but certainly not with any absolute innovations or peculiarities either in the vocabulary or the grammar. In the case of Chaucer we have the most conclusive evidence that he wrote the common English of his day in the identity of his language in all essential respects with that of other writers who were his contemporaries.

Moreover, by comparing him and his contemporaries with their predecessors and their followers, it is found that the changes undergone by the language exhibit only its natural progress under the operation of its inherent principles or tendencies.

The English of the age of Chaucer, being the earlier part of the Middle or Transitional Period of the language in its modified form, though reduced or restored to considerable regularity, has evidently not yet attained its final shape and structure, but is still in a state of growth or movement under two tendencies which had been for some time previous at work in it, and had brought it to its actual condition:—the first, a tendency to drop more of the ancient native tongue; the second, a tendency to assume more from the French.

I. The tendency to retreat still farther from the native tongue is evinced by the gradual loosening and falling off of such of the signs or vestiges of the old inflectional system as had not yet been quite got rid of, as well as by the continued disappearance of Teutonic vocables.

Thus :—the original termination of the infinitive, which had been already attenuated from *an* to *en*, is now often reduced to *e; e. g.* the original *spaecan*, or *specan* (to speak), which had already in the previous stage of the language become *speken*, is now frequently written (and was, probably, still more frequently pronounced) *speke* (in two syllables).

In the present indicative the singular is only slightly altered from -*e*, -*ast*, -*ath*, to -*e*, -*est*, -*eth* (*lufige, lufast, lufath*, becoming *lov-e, lov-est, lov-eth*) ; but the termination of the plural persons, which had been originally *ath*, and had been first changed into *eth*, is now often further softened or shortened into *en; e. g.* the original *we, ge, hi, lufiath*, had become *we, ye, hi,* or *they loveth,* or *loven.* Trevisa commonly has *loveth;* Chaucer and Mandeville, *loven.* In the second person plural of the imperative, the *eth* (which also had been originally *ath*) was some-times shortened, not into *en*, but into *e,—loveth ye,* or *love ye.**

---

* The second person singular of the imperative may probably be re-garded as being the verb in its elementary or most naked form. Such, at least, has always been the case in English. Thus, in Chaucer :—

> " Our hoste saw that he was dronken of ale,
> And sayd, *Abide*, Robin, my leve brother."
> > *Cant. Tales,* 3131.

> " The Reeve answered and saide, *Stint* thy clappe."
> > *Ibid.* 3146.

> " *Say* forth thy tal?, and *tarry* not the time."
> > *Ibid.* 3903.

But both in this and in the other moods, as at present, the second person plural, with its proper pronoun, is commonly used in a singular sense; as :—

> "Now *telleth ye,* Sire Monk, if that ye conne,
> Somewhat to quiten with the Knightes tale."
> > *Cant. Tales,* 3121.

The termination of the present participle, originally *ende*, has now, for the most part, passed into the more rapidly pronounceable *ing*, though it is still sometimes found as *ende* or *end*, *ande* or *and*, *ente* or *ent*, *ante* or *ant*.

Finally, the termination *e*, both in the verb and in other parts of speech, even while it continued to be written, was beginning to be dropped in the pronunciation; and in some words it was occasionally omitted in writing. According to Mr Guest (*Eng. Rhythms*, i. 34), the word *hire* is always a monosyllable with Chaucer, whether it represents the Anglo-Saxon *hire* (her), or *heora* (their); and the *e*, he adds, "was also lost in other cases when it followed *r*, and, *perhaps*, when it followed other letters." In the first and third persons singular of the preterite of verbs, again, which regularly terminated in *ede* (the entire tense running, *I lovede, thou lovedest, he lovede, we loveden, ye loveden, they loveden*), the *e* was beginning to be occasionally, though rarely, omitted (thus, *I loved, he loved*, as at present).

It is admitted that in the earliest form of the language the termination *e* made always a distinct syllable, as much as *a* or *u*. And this appears to be the case also in the prosody of Chaucer, except only in a very few words, in which, as just observed, the *e* had by his time begun to be dropt in the pronunciation, although it was still retained in writing. The only other circumstances in which it counts for nothing are when it is elided in consequence of the following word beginning with a vowel. *Ed* and *es* in like manner certainly were then in all cases pronounced as distinct syllables; thus, *lov-es, lov-ed, lov-ed-est, lov-ed-en*.

But many words also were then written with a final *e* which have now lost that termination.

It follows, therefore, that a great many words at this

stage of the language had a syllable more than the same
words now have. In some cases the final *e*, which con-
stituted the syllable in question, has disappeared only in
the pronunciation; in other cases it has disappeared entirely, not only in our speech but in our writing.

It does not seem to be disputed that Tyrwhitt has
given a correct account of the origin of one class of these
lost final *e*'s. "With respect to words imported directly
from France," he observes, "it is certainly quite natural
to suppose that for some time they retained their native
pronunciation." Thus such a word as *hoste* would continue to be both written with an *e* final (called *e* feminine)
and to be pronounced as a dissyllable, as it was in French,
and as its modern representative, *hôte*, still is, at least in
verse and in the more formal style of elocution. It is to
be supposed that in the anglicised word the final *e* was
first dropt in the pronunciation and then retrenched in
the spelling. In other words, again, borrowed from the
French, the *e*, though dropt in the pronunciation, has
been retained in the spelling, usually with the view of indicating a particular way of sounding a preceding vowel
or consonant; as in *large*, where it softens the *g*, or
in *face*, where it both softens the *c* and gives its name
sound to the *a*.

"We have not, indeed," Tyrwhitt proceeds to say, "so
clear a proof of the original pronunciation of the Saxon
part of our language; but we know, from general observ-
ation, that all changes of pronunciation are usually made
by small degrees; and, therefore, when we find that a
great number of those words which in Chaucer's time
ended in *e* originally ended in *a*, we may reasonably pre-
sume that our ancestors first passed from the broader
sound of *a* to the thinner sound of *e* feminine, and not at
once from *a* to *e* mute. Besides, if the final *e* in such

words was not pronounced, why was it added? From the time that it has confessedly ceased to be pronounced, it has been gradually omitted in them, except where it may be supposed of use to lengthen or soften the preceding syllable,—as in *hope, name,* &c. But, according to the ancient orthography, it terminates many words of Saxon original where it cannot have been added for any such purpose, as *herte, childe, olde, wilde,* &c. In these, therefore, we must suppose that it was pronounced as an *e* feminine, and made part of a second syllable; and so, by a parity of reason, in all others in which, as in these, it appears to have been substituted for the Saxon *a*." In a note he adds:—"In most of the words in which the final *e* has been omitted its use in lengthening or softening the preceding syllable has been supplied by an alteration in the orthography of that syllable. Thus, in *grete, mete, stele, rede, dere,* in which the first *e* was originally long, as closing a syllable, it has, since they have been pronounced as monosyllables, been changed either into *ea*, as in *great, meat, steal, read, dear,* or into *ee*, as in *greet, meet, steel, reed, deer.* In like manner, the *o* in *bote, fole, dore, gode, mone,* has been changed either into *oa*, as in *boat, foal,* or into *oo*, as in *door, good, moon.*"

It is only a part of this view of the origin of the *e* final in words even of native extraction that has been controverted. It is not denied that Tyrwhitt is right in regard to such words as in their original form ended either in *e* or in some other vowel which was equally represented by *e* in Early and Middle English. The only dispute is about such words as *herte, bote, gode,* &c., referred to by Tyrwhitt in the two last sentences of the passage above quoted, and in the annexed note.

The theory of the late Mr Price is that the *e* in such cases was an addition made by the Norman scribes, or disciples of the Norman school of writing, for the purpose of marking or indicating according to their principle of orthography that elongation of the preceding vowel which in the native English system was denoted by an accentual mark. Thus, for example, what in English orthography was *gód* was in Norman *gode;* what in the former was *líf,* was in the latter *life;* "and hence," concludes Mr Price, "the majority of those *e's* mute upon which Mr Tyrwhitt has expended so much unfounded speculation." * Tyrwhitt can hardly be said to have expended any speculation upon the particular class of words which Mr Price thus seeks to explain.

The question has been since examined more at length by Mr Guest. It was, according to Mr Guest, a fundamental rule of ancient English orthography to double the final consonant in an accented syllable when the vowel was a short one, that is, when it had what has been called the *shut* sound; and hence it came to be imagined that such a vowel should be followed and denoted by the doubling of the consonant, whether the syllable was accented or no. This, as we have seen, appears to have been the principle which Ormin followed, only regulating his spelling in conformity with it more uniformly or precisely than any other writer has done. But the old rule, Mr Guest conceives, also gave rise to another practice which has had a greater effect in deranging the orthography of the language. As the doubling of the consonant indicated a short or shut vowel sound, it followed that a single consonant would be the mark of the long, or what has been called the *name* sound; in such words, for instance, as *mone* (the moon), *time* (time) *name* (name), that would be the sound of the vowel in

* See his edition of Warton's *History of English Poetry* (1824), *Preface* (114), and vol. i. p. cii.

the first syllable. "Now, in the Anglo-Saxon," the statement proceeds, "there was a great number of words which had, as it were, two forms; one ending in a consonant, the other in a vowel. In the time of Chaucer, all the different vowel-endings were represented by the *e* final; and so great is the number of words which this writer uses sometimes as monosyllables, and sometimes as dissyllables with the addition of the *e*, that he has been accused of adding to the number of his syllables whenever it suited the convenience of his rhythm. In his works we find *hert* and *herte, bed* and *bedde, erth* and *erthe*, &c. In the Anglo-Saxon we find corresponding duplicates, the additional syllable giving to the noun in almost every case a new declension, and in most a new gender. In some few cases the final *e* had become mute even before the time of Chaucer; and it was wholly lost in the period which elapsed between his death and the accession of the Tudors. ·Still, however, it held its ground in our manuscripts, and *ure* (our), *rose* (a rose), &c., though pronounced as monosyllables, were still written according to the old spelling. Hence, it came gradually to be considered as a rule that, when a syllable ended in a single consonant and mute *e*, the vowel was long." Mr Guest has no doubt whatever that this is the origin of the very peculiar mode of indicating the long vowel which prevails in English orthography. To Mr Price's notion that the mode of spelling in question was the work of the Normans, he objects that the final *e*, which Mr Price conceives to have been annexed merely to denote the long vowel, or to be a substitute for the accentual mark of the native system, was *not* mute in Norman French.—(*Eng. Rhythms*, i. 109.)

It is not quite clear whether in Mr Guest's view there are any cases in which the *e* may be supposed to have had nothing corresponding to it in the Original English word, and to have been affixed merely to denote that the preceding vowel had the long or name sound after it had come, in the way that has been explained, to be a received rule of pronunciation that that was the sound to be borne by a vowel whenever it was followed by a single consonant and an *e*. Mr Price appears to have considered the final *e* generally to have originated in this way; and in that notion he probably held it a mistake to imagine that it had ever been pronounced as a distinct syllable.*

One result, Mr Guest goes on to observe, of this employment of the final *e* mute to indicate a long vowel was to save many of our monosyllables from the duplication of the final consonant. The mere absence of the *e* would be held to imply that the vowel had its short or shut sound. Having the name sound in *white, pate*, and *rote*, it would have the shut sound in *whit, pat*, and *rot*.

Mr Guest holds that there have been four systems employed at different periods to mark the quantity (in reference at least to the more recent stages of the language we ought rather to say the quality) of our English vowels. 1. In the so-called Anglo-Saxon or original form of the language the long time was properly marked by the acute accent: thus, *gód* (good) was distinguished from *God* (God). 2. Next it came to be marked in many instances by the doubling of the vowel: thus *gód* was written *good* (perhaps originally pronounced as we

---

* Mr Price's views were to have been more fully explained in a volume which was announced in his edition of *Warton* as shortly to be published, but which has never appeared, entitled " Illustrations of Warton's History of English Poetry; containing . . . . . An Examination of Mr Tyrwhitt's Essay on the Language and Versification of Chaucer," &c.

now pronounce *goad*). 3. The long or name sound was indicated simply by leaving the following consonant single; thus, Ormin probably intended his *shep* to be sounded *sheep*. 4. The same effect was produced by the mute *e*. And our modern practice, Mr Guest thinks, is to a certain extent a combination, or rather a confusion, of the three last systems. (*Eng. Rhythms*, i. 110.)

It is never to be forgotten, in the consideration of this subject, that every one of our English vowel letters represents, in our established system of orthography, not only different quantities of the same sound, but totally different sounds. After the explanations we have quoted, Mr Guest proceeds:—" We have hitherto denominated certain vowels long and short, as though we considered the only difference between them to be their time; as, though, for instance, the vowel in *meet* differed from that in *met* only in its being longer. The truth is, they are of widely different quality. The spelling of many words has remained unchanged for a period during which we have the strongest evidence of a great change in our pronunciation. When the orthography of the words *meet* and *met* was settled, the vowels in all probability differed only in respect of time; but they have now been changing for some centuries, till they have nothing in common between them but a similarity in their spelling."

The assumption that sounds which are represented by the same letter are always either the same or differ only in quantity is what has most perplexed the treatment of this subject. The fact is, that in some cases the sounds are totally different in kind. Even the *a* in *fan*, the *a* in *bath*, and the *a* in *was*, are, strictly speaking, all distinguishable in quality, though perhaps nearly related, and having a tendency to pass into one another; the same may be said of the *o* in *note*, and the *o* in *hog* (which,

again, is the same sound in quality or kind with that of
the *a* in *was*), and perhaps of the *u* in *but*, and the *u* in
full (the same essentially with the *oo* in *good*), and the *u*
in *tune* (which is otherwise represented by *ew*, as in *pew;*
by *ue*, as in *due;* by *eau*, as in *beauty;* and, it may be, in
other ways). But the sound of *a* in *pane* (the same,
only longer, with that of *e* in *pen*) is totally different
from the sound given to the same letter in *pan*. So is
the sound of *e* in *men* from its sound in *me*. So, finally,
is the sound of *i* in *pin* from its sound in *pine*. In all
these cases the difference is one not merely of length, or
not of length at all, but of quality or kind; and the two
sounds are fully as distinct, or as wide apart, as any two
vowel sounds in the language.

The English way of reading Latin is to read it exactly
as English is read. For instance, the long *a* in *orator*,
being the accented syllable (as the penult always is when
long), is sounded like the *a* in *pane;* but the equally
long *a* in *oratoris*, not having the accent upon it, is
sounded like the *a* in *pan*. The vowel is treated in the
two words exactly as it is in the two English words
oration and *oratory*. The effect of this system is that,
at least in all penults (although not always in other
syllables), a long *a* is pronounced like the *a* in *pane*,
a long *e* like the *e* in *me*, and a long *i* like the *i* in *pine;*
while a short *a* takes commonly the sound of *a* in
pan, a short *e* that of *e* in *net*, and a short *i* that of *i*
in *pin*.

English writers upon the subject of pronunciation
have thus been very generally led to assume that the two
sounds, connected in these several cases by being represented by the same letter, are similarly connected as corresponding long and short sounds in nature. There is
scarcely a disquisition on the subject to be found in the

language which is not more or less tainted with this fal-
lacy. Even where it is perceived and admitted that the
two sounds differ in kind, or, in other words, that they
are quite distinct sounds, a notion or half notion is still
apt to lurk, both in the nomenclature and in the reasoning, that the one is naturally the short sound of the
other.

The fact is, that, in so far as respects mere length, the
sounds in question can hardly be characterised as distinguishable into two sets. At any rate, a syllable, the
vowel sound in which is what is called the short *a*, *e*,
or *i*, may certainly be made to occupy, and often does
occupy, as much time in the enunciation as one in which
the vowel sound is what is called the long *a*, *e*, or *i*.
Every classical scholar, indeed, is familiar with one form
of this fact, in the prolongation of a short vowel in the
Greek and Latin by what is called position, or the circumstance of its being followed by two consonants. Even
in these ancient languages, however, it is worth noting
that, while position makes a short vowel long, or, as we
are told, doubles its time, it is not held, at least in pro-
sodical effect, to make a long vowel e'ther twice as long,
or any longer at all. But in English, two things are remarkable in connexion with this matter:—1. That, upon
any definition or understanding of the terms *long* and
short that can be proposed, what is called a short vowel,
or the syllable in which it stands, may be long without
position; 2. That such a vowel or syllable may be short
with or notwithstanding position.

Here again, however, English scholars have almost
universally been blinded to the plainest facts in their
own language by their classical preconceptions. Because
a vowel followed by two consonants is long in Greek and
Latin, it has been commonly assumed that it is always

long in a similar position in English too. And this unfounded notion has been productive of the greater confusion, inasmuch as it runs directly counter to the other prejudice just adverted to, which holds the sound that a vowel commonly has in this situation to be short. Thus, for example, while the monosyllable *win* is held to be short, the same combination of letters, retaining precisely the same sound, when it comes to form the first syllable of the word *winter*, is half regarded as long; and that although it is hardly pretended that any more time is taken to pronounce it in the one case than in the other.

In truth, however the matter may stand in Latin, in English some of the syllables that would be accounted long under the rule of position are among the slightest and shortest in the language; such, for instance, as the conjunction *and*, and the terminations *ant* and *ent*. In regard to this point there can be no doubt that the pronunciation of the one language is constructed upon a different principle from that of the other. Whatever may be the true nature of the distinction between what are denominated long and short syllables, which is unquestionably the basis of Latin prosody and Latin verse, it is certain that a vowel standing in position, and the syllable containing that vowel, are uniformly ranked with and treated as belonging prosodically to one of the two classes into which all vowels and syllables are divided,—namely, to that which is described as long. It is possible that by the terms *long* and *short* the ancient grammarians may have meant nothing more than accented and unaccented. All that is necessary to be affirmed here is, that accent is, at any rate, the sole principle of English prosody and of English verse. And in English a syllable of which the vowel is in position is by no means necessarily an accented syllable, or one having prosodically the force of such.

Mr Guest believes that the *e* final in Chaucer and other writers of the same age is frequently the *e* or *a* of inflection of the original form of the language. Thus, in the opening couplet of the *Canterbury Tales,*—

> " Whanne that April with his shoures sote
> The drought of March had perced to the rote,"

he holds the *e* of *sote* to be the sign of the plural, and the *e* of *rote* to be most probably the sign of the dative singular; the common form of the original word for *root* being *rot*. Again, he conceives that in the following verse,

> " Hire gretest othe n'as but by Seint Loy,"

othe represents the ancient genitive plural *atha;* so that *hire gretest othe* means *her greatest of oaths.* In support of this interpretation he adduces from the *Geste of King Horn* the expression "Riche menne sones " (that is, *sons of rich men*) ; from *Piers Plowman*, that of "poure menne cotes" (*poor men's cots*); and from Gower's *Confessio Amantis*, that of "her horse knave" (*their horses groom*).* Moreover, he looks upon the final *e* of the adjective as being not only the sign of the plural (as in *shoures sote*), and the mark of what is called the definite declension, or the form which the adjective takes after *the*, or *this*, or *that*, or a possessive pronoun (as in *the gret-e see*, and *this sik-e man*, and *hire whit-e voluper-e*, that is, *her white cap*), but the affixed *e* which in the Original English con-

* *Eng. Rhythms,* i. 30—33.

verted an adjective into an adverb. Thus, in the line from the *Clerke's Tale*, in the *Canterbury Tales*,

"And in a cloth of gold that bright-e shone,"

he regards *bright-e* as representing, not our present adjective *bright*, but our adverb *brightly*. In the superlative, however, he observes, it is not the adverb, but the adjective, that takes the *e ;* in other words, that *brightest* is *brighteste*, and that *brightliest* is *brightest*.*

The full account, then, of that most remarkable among the peculiarities which distinguish the English of Chaucer from that of the present day, the *e* terminating so many of his words, and always forming a syllable, which has now disappeared altogether from the pronunciation, and in great part from the spelling, of the language, may be comprised in the five following propositions :—

1. In words borrowed from the French it is, as pointed out by Tyrwhitt, the *e* feminine of that language, still universally retained both in French orthography and French prosody, though in English it has ceased to be pronounced, and only continues to be written where its presence is necessary to indicate the sound of a preceding vowel or consonant.

2. In nouns of native origin it is, in many cases, as

---

* *Eng. Rhythms*, i. 29. The example that Mr Guest gives of this last canon is the following line in the *Prologue* to the *Canterbury Tales :*—

"And fro the time that he *firste* began."

And so, indeed, the line is printed by Tyrwhitt. But it is evident that, according to the canon, *firste* ought to be *first*. And that amendment is also required by the prosody, if, as is believed to be the case, the final *e* in Chaucer always (except in *hire*, and, it may be, two or three other words) makes a distinct syllable when the following word begins with a consonant.

also pointed out by Tyrwhitt, the substitute for, or remnant of, the ancient nominative singular termination (which was either *e*, or *a*, or *u*).

3. In other native nouns, according to Mr Guest, it is the *e* or *a* of the old dative singular, or genitive plural, or nominative plural in adjectives, or the sign of the definite form of the adjective, or of the adverb as distinguished from the adjective, or of the superlative of the adjective as distinguished from the superlative of the adverb.

4. In the verb, as pointed out by Tyrwhitt, it is the termination, in the stage at which the language had arrived through the decay of the ancient grammatical system, of the first person singular of the present indicative and the first and third persons singular of the perfect, and of one form of the second person plural of the imperative, and one form of the infinitive.

5. In many words of native derivation, howsoever it may have originated—whether from some primitive form, or, as Mr Price conceives, merely in an orthographical expedient—it probably gave the *name* sound to a preceding vowel, or served to indicate that it had such sound; being itself, however, at the same time a distinct syllable in this as well as in all other cases.

The other principal peculiarities that distinguish the grammar of Chaucer's English from that of the English of the present day are the following:—

The substantive verb *to ben* (our *to be*) was inflected in the singular of the present indicative as it still is; but the form throughout the plural was *aren* or *ben*. So in the imperfect the plural form was *weren*.

Our *to have* was *to haven*, or *to han*, which in the present was inflected by *have*, *havest* or *hast*, *haveth* or *hath* for the singular, and by *haven* or *han* for the plural; and in the imperfect by *hadde, haddest, hadde* for the singular, and *hadden* for the plural.

They then said *shal* in the singular, but *shullen* in the plural, of the present; *shulde* in the singular, and *shulden* in the plural, of the imperfect.

In the present they said *wil* or *wol* in the singular, *willen* or *wollen* in the plural; in the imperfect, *wolde* in the singular, *wolden* in the plural.

In the present they said *can* or *con* in the singular and *connen* in the plural; in the imperfect, *coude* in the singular, and *couden* in the plural. Our established spelling of *could* with an *l* has arisen from its being assumed by mistake that its original form was similar to those of *should* and *would*.

May then made in the present *may* or *mow* in the singular, and *mowen* in the plural; in the imperfect, *moughte* or *mighte* in the singular, *moughten* or *mighten* in the plural.

The first personal pronoun was generally *I*, as at present, but sometimes *Ich*, or *Iche*; in the plural of the pronoun of the second person *ye* was always used for the nominative, *you* for the accusative; our *they* was sometimes *hi*; *them* was usually *hem* (nearly the same with our present colloquial *'em*, which little more than a century ago was commonly used also in writing); and *their* was usually *hire*, which (pronounced in all its senses as a monosyllable) was also the form both for the adjective pronoun *her* and for the accusative of the personal pronoun *she*.

II. The tendency of the English of the age of Chaucer to approximate still more to the French is indicated by the continued adoption of new words of French extrac-

tion, often in substitution for native ones; and this process goes on, for the most part at an accelerating rate, to
about the end of the fifteenth century.

No additional words were now borrowed or revived from
the English of the period before the Conquest.

Of the words used by Chaucer and the other writers
of that time which have now become obsolete, some indeed are French, but the greater number are of native
growth. This fact, while it indicates the tendency of the
language, or of its vocabulary, goes also to corroborate
the probability that Chaucer, in the extent to which he
employed words of French origin, only followed, and did
not by any means go beyond, the demand of the time,
and the natural movement of the language.

Out of the practice of borrowing words from the
French there grew another of fabricating similar words
directly from the Latin, the great source of the French.
In this way many words of Latin formation found their
way into the English which the French had never possessed, but which were all constructed nevertheless upon
the model of those that had been received through the
medium of that language. Thus, for example, every such
word formed from a Latin substantive in *tio* was made to
end in *tion*, and every one formed from a Latin substantive in *itas* in *ity* (after the French *ité*).

These are the *aureate terms*, their pedantic and excess-
ive employment of which Campbell (*Essay on English
Poetry*, xlviii.) objects in particular against the Scottish
versifiers of the fifteenth century, the generality of whom,
he observes, " when they meant to be most eloquent, tore
up words from the Latin, which never took root in the
language, like children making a mock garden with flowers
and branches stuck in the ground, which speedily wither."

But, although many of the words thus transplanted from the French and Latin never effected a cohesion with the soil of the language, and some may perhaps never have been used except by the writer who introduced them, many took firm root, and they now constitute a large and indispensable portion of our national speech. Among them are all our substantives ending in *tion* and *sion*; all those in *ity*; all in *ance* and *ancy*, *ence* and *ency*, with their connected adjectives in *ant* and *ent*; most of those in *ment* (for some are hybrids, made up of this Latin termination annexed to an English root); all in *tor*, *tory*, and *ure*; all adjectives in *ary* and *ory*, in *ic* and *ical*, in *ive*, *ile*, and *ible*, and most of those in *able*; and all verbs in *ate*, *act*, *ect*, *ict*, and *fy*; besides various smaller classes of words.*

Dr Latham (*English Language*, 3rd edit., 101) describes what he designates the *Latin of the Third Period*, or that which was introduced between the Norman Conquest and the revival of literature (which for England may be understood to mean the beginning of the sixteenth century), as having " chiefly originated with the monks, in the universities, and, to a certain extent, in the courts of law." But the fact is, that most of the words of Latin or French derivation, which found their way into the language in this interval, were introduced by the authors of the most popular literature of the day.

---

* The most complete examination to which the English language has been subjected with a view to the determination of the proportion which its vocabulary contains of Latin or French is that which it has received in a little work by Dr J. P. Thommerel, entitled " Recherches sur la Fusion du Franco-Normand et de l'Anglo-Saxon," Paris, 1841. I have discussed this question in the Second of a series of papers entitled " Curiosities of the English Language," published in the *Dublin University Magazine* for October 1857.

Perhaps it would be better not to distinguish this *Latin
of the Third Period* from what Dr Latham calls the *Latin
of the Fourth Period*, or that introduced between the revival of literature and the present time, but to regard the
latter as only a continuation of the former. Up to about
the commencement of the sixteenth century French and
Latin may be said to have flowed into the language in a
stream, or to have been drunk up by it as if it were
athirst; but about that date the point of saturation would
seem to have been reached, or the appetite of absorption
to have been quenched: it has since received only single
words, as occasion arose.

The unripe or unconsolidated condition of the language,
more especially at the commencement of the period of
Middle English, or of its passage from Early English to
Modern English, is indicated by the fluctuating accentuation of many of the words it was then appropriating from
the French. Chaucer has, for instance, in one place *virtúe*,
in another *vírtue*; in one place *natúre*, in another *náture*;
in one place *langáge*, in another *lángage*; the first of the
two modes of accentuation in each case being the French,
the second the English one. For some time probably
the former would be the more prevalent; but ultimately
all these imported words adopted the English accentuation, and entirely lost their native one; thus showing
that the predominant genius of the language in its music,
as well as in its grammar, was still English.

Latin, either in its original state, or transformed into
French, is the only foreign element with which the
Gothic basis of our language has combined to any large
extent.

In modern times, it is true, a vast number of scientific

and technical terms have been fabricated from the Greek; and this is the only manufacture of additions to our vocabulary upon a considerable scale that still goes on. But such words do not belong to the flesh and blood of the language at all; they may be styled its non-natural part, or an artificial appendage to it; they stand in the same relation to its proper substance in which the tools that a man works with stand to his living person.

XX. Confining ourselves to the history of the English language since the Norman Conquest, we may call the First Century after that date its Infancy; the Second its childhood; the Third its Boyhood; the Fourth and Fifth its Youth, or Adolescence; and the time that has since elapsed its Manhood. , Its Infancy and Childhood will thus correspond with what is usually designated the Period of Semi-Saxon; its Boyhood with that of Early English; its Youth with that of Middle English; its Manhood with that of Modern English.

IT is evident, from what has been stated in the preceding Sections, that the only natural, or scientific, division of the history of the English language in its entire extent is into the three following stages:—

1. That of its original form, when it retained intact both the integrity of its Grammar (or inflectional system) and the homogeneousness of its Vocabulary; being that in which it subsisted during the period preceding the Norman Conquest, and in which it is commonly spoken of by modern philologists under the name of the Saxon, or Anglo-Saxon;

2. That of its degradation into an illiterate patois by the breaking up of its Grammar, though without the intrusion of any foreign element into its Vocabulary (corresponding to what is commonly called the Semi-Saxon); being that in which it is found for the first two centuries after the Conquest;

3. That of its acquisition of both a new form and a new spirit or genius by the combination of the original Gothic basis of its Vocabulary with a Latin (Romance, Norman, or French) element; being that in which it still is, and comprehending the periods usually called those of Early English, of Middle English, and of Modern English.

The three successive and distinct states or forms may be most properly designated:—the First, that of Pure or Simple English; the Second, that of Broken or Semi-English; the Third, that of Mixed or Compound English.*

But the following Table gives us a convenient enough technical division (convenient to be known, at any rate, as being that currently assumed) of so much of the history of the language as is subsequent to the Norman Conquest, at which date it may be considered to have, as it were, started upon a new career:†—

* See this scheme of the true History of the Language explained and illustrated in Chapter First of "The Curiosities of the English Language," published in the *Dublin University Magazine* for July 1857.

† The dates in the Table are accommodated to the Kings' reigns; but the Periods and Ages may be most conveniently considered as extending from about the middle of one century to the middle of another, and as therefore consisting in each case of one or more centuries. And, of course, as with the human being to which it is compared, the language was making progress during or within each of the stages into which its history may be thus divided, as much as in passing from one to another of them.

THE ENGLISH LANGUAGE SINCE THE NORMAN CONQUEST.

Periods.	Reigns.	Dates.	Position in Relation to the French.	Ages.
I. Semi-Saxon : 206 years.	William I. William II. Henry I. Stephen.	A.D. 1066-1154	Suppressed and superseded.	Infancy: 88 years.
	Henry II. Richard I. John. Henry III.	1154-1272	In revolt.	Childhood: 118 years.
II. Early English : 105 years.	Edward I. Edward II. Edward III.	1272-1377	In ascendancy.	Boyhood: 105 years.
III. Middle English : 181 years.	Richard II. Henry IV. Henry V. Henry VI. Edward IV. Edward V. Richard III. Henry VII. Henry VIII. Edward VI. Mary.	1377-1558	In supremacy.	Youth: 181 years.
IV. Modern English.	Elizabeth, &c.	1558 ——	In sole dominion.	Manhood.

ILLUSTRATIVE SPECIMENS.

I. Original English; English Pure or Simple (Saxon, or Anglo-Saxon).

1. *From the Voyage of Ohther in Alfred's Translation of Orosius, Book i. :—before* A.D. 900.

And thær is mid Estum dheaw, thonne thær bidh man dead, thæt he lidh inne unforbærned mid his magum and freondum monadh, ge hwilum twegen, and tha kyningas and tha odhre heahdhungene men swa micle lencg swa hi maran speda habbadh; hwilum healf gear thæt hi beodh unforbærned, and licgadh bufan eorthan on hyra husum. And, ealle tha hwile the thæt lic bidh inne, thær sceal beon gedrync and plega, odh thone dæg the hi hine forbærnadh.

[And there is with Esthonians a custom, when there is one dead, that he lieth within unburnt with his kinsmen and friends a month, yea sometimes (whiles, *Scot.*) twain, and the kings and the other high-spoken-of men so much (mickle, *Scot.*) longer as they more wealth (*lit.* speed) have; sometimes [it is] half a year that they be unburnt, and lie above earth in their houses. And, all the while that the corpse is within, there shall be [it is the custom that there be] drinking and play until the day that they it burn.]

1 2

2. *From the latter portion of the Chronicle:—about* 1100.

A.D. 1087.— ... Dhissum thus gedone, se cyng Willelm cearde ongean to Normandige. . . He swealt on Normandige on thone nextan dæg æfter nativitas Sc̄e Marie; and man begyrgede hine on Cathum æt Sc̄e [Sc̄i?] Stephanes mynstre. . . Gif hwa gewilniged to gewitane hu gedon man he was, odhdhe hwilcne wurdh-scipe he hæfde, odhdhe hu fela lande he wære hlaford, thonne wille we be him awritan swa swa we hine ageaton; we him onlocodan, and odhre hwile on his hirede wunedon. . . He sætte mycel deorfridh, and he lægde laga thær widh; thæt swa hwa swa sloge heort odhdhe hinde thæt hine man sceold blendian. He forbead tha heortas,* swylce eac tha baras. Swa swidhe he lufode tha heodeor swylce he wære heora fæder. Eac he sætte be tham haran thæt hi mosten freo faran. His rice men hit mæn-don, and tha earme men hit beceorodan; ac he wæs swa stidh thæt he ne rohte heora eallra nidh.

[This thus done, the King William turned again to Normandy. . . He died in Normandy on the next day after (the) nativity of St Mary (*Nativitas Sanctæ Mariæ*); and man (Ger. *man*, Fr. *on*, anciently *homme*) buried him in Caen, at St Stephen's minster. . . If any may wish to know how to do man (what kind of man) he was, or what worship he had, or of how many lands he was lord, then will we by (in regard to) him write so as we him knew: we him beheld, and other while in his household wonned (dwelt) . . . He set much deer free-ground (he made many deer-parks), and he laid (down) laws therewith; that whoso slew hare or hind that him man should blind. As he forbade

---

* We ought, apparently, to read—*thæt hwa swa sloge heort,* and *Swa he forbead tha heortas.* The passage, from *He sætte mycel deor-fridh* is probably in rhyme, although Dr Ingram's proposed substitu-tion of *blinde* for *blendian* is inadmissible without a verb in the in-finitive after *sceold.*

[to slay] the harts, so also the boars. So much he loved the high-deer as he were their father. Also he set by (appointed regarding) the hares that they must free fare. His rich men it moaned, and the poor men it lamented; but he was so stern, that he recked not the hatred of them all.]

The element printed *dh* in these two extracts is to be sounded as the *h* in *this*. It is represented in the MSS., and in the common so-called Saxon printing, by one character; as the *th* heard in *thin* is by another. But there is by no means a perfect correspondence, as to this matter, between the old language and our present English; nor, indeed, are the two characters distinguished with any uniformity of usage in the MSS.

II.   Broken English, or Semi-English (Semi-Saxon):
A.D. 1050—1250.

3. *The Commencement of Layamon's Brut, according to
the oldest of the two Versions, MS. Cott. Calig. A. ix.:
—about* 1200.*

An preost wes on leoden;
Layamon wes ihoten;
He wes Leovenadhes sone :
' Lidhe him beo Drihtē.
He wonede at Ernleye,
At ædhelen are chirechen,
Uppen Sevarne stalhe:
Sel thar him thuhte;
On fest Radestone ;
Ther he bock radde.
Hit com him on mode,
And on his mern thonke,
Thet he wolde of Engle
Tha ædhelæn tellen;
Wat heo ihoten weoren,
And wonene heo comen,
Tha Englene londe
Ærest ahten

---

* In this and other Extracts the ancient fashion of writing and printing *i* for *j*, *u* for *v*, and *v* for *u*, in particular circumstances, has not
been adhered to, though preserved by some of the modern editors.   It
is merely a different mode of forming the letters in question, which
cannot be supposed to have affected their sound.

Æfter than flode,
The from Drihtene com,
The al her a-quelde
Quic that he funde,
Buten Noe and Sem,
Japhet and Cham,
And heore four wives,
The mid heom weren on archen.

[A priest was on earth (or, perhaps, in the land, or among the people) ; Layamon was [he] (called); he was Leovenath's son; gracious to him be [the] Lord. He wonned (dwelt) at Ernley, at a noble church, upon Severn's bank,—good there to him [it] seemed— near Radestone ; there he book read. It came to him in mind, and in his chief (?) thought, that he would of Englishmen the noble-deeds tell ; what they called were, and whence they came, that English land first owned, after the flood, that from [the] Lord came, that all here quelled (destroyed), quick (alive) that it found, but Noah and Shem, Japheth and Ham, and their four wives, that with them were in [the] ark.]

In the later version, MS. Cott. Otho, C. xiii., the passage stands thus :—

A prest was in londe ;
Laweman was hote ;
He was Leucais sone :
Lef him beo drifte.
He wonede at Ernleie,
Wid than gode cnithte ;
Uppen Sevarne ;
Merie ther him thohte ;
Faste bi Radistone :
Ther heo bokes radde.
Hit com him on mode,
And on his thonke,

That he wolde of Engelond
The riftnesse telle ;
Wat the men hi-hote weren,
And wancne hi comen,
The Englene lond
Ærest afden
After than flode,
That fram God com ;
That al ere acwelde
Cwic that hit funde,
Bot Noe and Sem,
Japhet and Cam,
And hire four wifes,
That mid ham there weren.

In this version Sir F. Madden conjectures that *hote*, in line 2, should
be *ihote ;* that *heo*, in line 10, should be *he ;* and that *wancne*, in line
16, should be *wanene.*

---

4. *Layamon's Description* (with the two hemistichs, or
short lines, printed as a single verse) *of the arming
of Prince Arthur before the Battle of Baddon Hill,
or Bath (A.D.* 520 ?), *from the Brut,* 21,149—
21,168 ; *Madden,* II. 464-5 :—*also given, with one or
two variations, by Guest, Eng. Rh.* II. 118, 119 :—
from MS. Cott. Calig. A. ix :—about 1200.

He heng an his sweore ænne sceld deore ;
His nome was on Bruttisc Pridwen ihaten :
Ther was innen igraven mid rede golde staven
An on-licnes deore of Drihtenes moder.
His spere he·nom an honde, tha Ron wes ihaten.
Tha he hafden al his iweden tha leop he on his steden.

Tha he mihte behalden tha bihalves stoden
Thene væireste cniht the verde scolde leden;
Ne isæh nævere na man selere cniht nenne
Thenne him wes Ardhur, adhelest cunnes."

That is, literally :—

He hung on his neck a dear [precious] shield;
Its name was in British called Pridwen :
There was within [on it] engraven with red gold tracings
A dear likeness of the Lord's mother.
His spear he took in hand, that was called Ron.
When he had all his weeds [accoutrements], then leapt he on his
     steed.
Then they might behold that beside stood
The fairest knight that host should lead;
Nor saw never no man better knight none
Than he was, Arthur, noblest of kin.

In the later version, MS Cott. OtLo, C. xiii. (1250?), this passage
stands :—

He heng on his swere one sceald deore ;
His name was in Bruttisse Pridewyn ihote;
That (thar?) was hine igraved on anlichnesse of golde,
That was mid isothe Drihtene moder.
His spere he nam an honde, that Ron was ihote.
Tho he hadde al his wede, tho leop he on his stede.
Tho hii mihte bi-holde that thar bi-halves were
Thane fairest cniht that ferde sal leade.

(The two concluding lines do not occur in the later MS.)

The y which occurs in *Layamon*, *Ernleye*, and some other words,
stands for a character in the original the form of which, as well as its
position, would seem to indicate that it represented a sound com-

bining that of *g* and *y*, or intermediate between the two. In the modern language it has for the most part become *y* before a vowel, and *g* hard, or *gh*, elsewhere. It never can have had any resemblance to the sound of *z*, by which it has sometimes been ignorantly rendered in modern reprints of old English and Scottish texts. In the later version of Layamon this character appears much less frequently than in the earlier version, and that representing *dh* does not occur at all.

III. Compound English; A.D. 1250—(Early English; 1250—1350).

5. *Dedication by the Author of the Ormulum to his Brother:—about* 1260 ?

Nu, brotherr Wallterr, brotherr min affterr the flaeshess kinde;

And brotherr min i Crisstenndom thurrh fulluhht and thurrh trowwthe;

And brotherr min i Godess hus, yet o the thride wise,

Thurrh thatt witt hafenn takenn ba an reghellboc to follghenn,

Unnderr kanunnkess had and lif, swa summ Sannt Awwstin sette;

Icc hafe don swa summ thu badd, and fortheddte thin wille;

Icc hafe wennd inntill Ennglissh goddspelless halghe lare,

Affterr thatt little witt tatt me min Drihhten hafethth lenedd.

[Now, brother Walter, brother mine after the flesh's kind;
And brother mine in Christendom, through baptism and through truth (faith);
And brother mine in God's house, yet in the third wise,
Through (for) that we have taken both one rule-book to follow,
Under (the) canon's rank and life so as Saint Austin ruled ;
I have done so as thou badest, and furthered thy will (wish) ;
I have turned into English [the] Gospel's holy lore,
After that little wit that me my Lord hath lent.]

---

6. *The Commencement of Robert of Gloucester's Chronicle, as printed by Hearne:—about* 1300.

Engelond ys a wel god lond, ich wene of eche lond best,
Yset in the ende of the world, as al in the West.

The see goth hym al a boute, he stont as an yle.
Here fon hco durre the lasse doute, but hit be thorw
 gyle
Of fol of the selve lond, as me hath y seye wyle.
From South to North he is long eighte hondred myle;
And foure hondred myle brod from Est to West to
 wende,
Amydde tho lond as yt be, and noght as by the on ende.
Plente me may in Engelond of alle gode y se,
Bute folc yt for gulte other yeres the worse be.
For Engelond ys ful ynow of fruyt and of tren,
Of wodes and of parkes, that joye yt ys to sen;
Of foules and of bestes, of wylde and tame al so;
Of salt fysch and eche fresch, and fayre ryveres ther to;
Of welles swete and colde ynow, of lesen and of mede;
Of selver or and of gold, of tyn and of lede;
Of stel, of yrn, and of bras; of god corn gret won
Of whyte and of wolle god, betere ne may be non.

[England is a very good land, I ween of every land [the] best; set
in the end of the world, as [being] wholly in the west. The sea goeth
it all about; it standeth as an isle. Their foes they need the less fear,
except it be through guile of folk of the same land, as one hath seen
sometimes. From South to North it is long eight hundred mile; and
four hundred mile broad from East to West to wend, amid the land as
it be, and not as by the one end. Plenty one may in England of all
good see, except (were it not for) folk that for guilt some years the
worse be. For England is full enough of fruit and of trees; of woods
and of parks, that joy it is to see; of fowls and of beasts, of wild and
tame also; of salt fish and eke fresh, and fair rivers thereto; of wells
sweet and cold enow, of pasture and of mead; of silver ore and of gold,
of tin and of lead; of steel, of iron, and of brass; of good corn great
store; of wheat and of good wool, better may be none.]

7. Robert de Brunne's Account of the Alteration of the Coinage by Edward I. in 1282, from his Translation of Peter Langtoft's Chronicle :—about 1340.

Now turnes Edward ageyn to London his cite,
And wille wite certeyn [1] who schent [2] has his mone.
Of clippers, of roungers,[3] of suilk [4] takes he questis;
Old used traitoures ilk at other hand kestis.
Ilk these other out said, ilk a schrewe other greves;[5]
Of fele [6] were handes laid, and hanged ther as theves.
Edward did smyte [7] rounde peny, halfpeny, ferthing,
The croise [8] passed the bounde of alle thorghout the ryng.
The kynge's side salle be the hede and his name writen;
The croyce side what cite it was in coyned and smyten.
The povere man ne the preste the peny prayses no thing.
Men gyf God the lest,[9] the fesse [10] him with a ferthing.
A thousand and two hundred and fourscore yeres mo,[11]
Of this mone men wondred first when it gan go.*

[1] Know certainly.　　[2] Corrupted.　　[3] Nippers.　　[4] Such.

[5] *Ilk* and *ilk a* mean *every* with De Brunne, as they still do in the Scottish dialect; and *kestis* is *casts ;* but, perhaps, scarcely more than a doubtful sense can be extracted from these two lines, as Hearne has printed them. His Glossary affords no aid towards their interpretation.

[6] Many.　　　　　　　　　　　　　[7] Strike.

[8] Cross (the *oi* or *oy* being probably pronounced nearly as our *o* in the modern form of the word, or somewhat as the *oi* in the French *croix*).

[9] Least.　　　　　[10] They feast.　　　　　[11] More.

* From Hearne's Edition, 238, 239.—Of course the *e* makes a distinct syllable in such words as *cite* and *mone.*

(Middle English. A.D. 1350—1550).

8. *Commencement of Minot's Poem on the Battle of Halidon Hill, fought* A.D. 1333 :—*about* 1350.

Trew king, that sittes in trone,
   Unto the I tell my tale,
And unto the I bid a bone [1]
   For thou ert bute [2] of all my bale :
Als thou made midelerd and the mone, [3]
   And bestes and fowles grete and smale,
Unto me send thi socore sone,
   And dresce my dedes in this dale. [4]

[1] Offer a prayer.   [2] Boot, remedy.
[3] As thou madest middle-earth and the moon.
[4] Direct my deeds in this vale (of misery).

---

9. *Commencement of the Vision of Piers Ploughman, from Wright's Edition,* 1842 :—*about* 1360.

In a somer seson
Whan softe was the sonne,
I shoop me into shroudes [1]
As I a sheep [2] weere,
In habite as an heremite
Unholy of werkes,

Went wide in this world
Wondres to here;
Ac[3] on a May morwenynge
On Malverne hilles
Me befel a ferly,[4]
Of fairye me thoghte.
I was wery[5] for-wandred,
And went me to reste
Under a brood[6] bank
By a bournes syde;
And as I lay and lenede,
And loked on the watres,
I slombred into a slepyng,
It sweyed so murye.[7]

[1] I put myself into clothes.   [2] Shepherd.
[3] And.   [4] Wonder.   [5] Weary.   [6] Broad.
[7] It sounded so pleasant.

---

10. *Commencement of the Seventh Chapter of Sir John Mandevil's Travels, entitled " Of the Pilgrimages in Jerusalem, and of the Holy Places thereaboute," from the Cotton MS. Titus, C. xvi., which is believed to have been written about the year* 1400:—*about* 1370.*

After for to speke of Jerusalem the holy cytee, yee schull undirstonde that it stont full faire betwene hilles, and there be no ryveres ne welles, but watar cometh by

* This text was first published in a contribution to the " Pictorial History of England " by Sir Henry Ellis.

condyte from Ebron. And yee schulle understonde that
Jerusalem of olde tyme, unto the tyme of Melchisedech,
was cleped Jebus; and after it was clept Salem, unto the
tyme of Kyng David, that put these two names to gider,
and cleped it Jerosolomye. And after that men cleped
it Jerusalem, and so it is cleped yit. And aboute Jerusalem is the kyngdom of Surrye (*Syria*). And there
besyde is the lond of Palestyne. And besyde it is Asco-
lon. And besyde that is the lond of Maritanie. But
Jerusalem is in the lond of Judee; and it is clept Jude
for that Judas Machabeus was kyng of that contree.
And it marcheth estward to the kyngdom of Araby; on
the south syde to the lond of Egipt; and on the west
syde to the Grete See. On the north syde toward the
kyngdom of Surrye, and to the see of Cypre.

---

11. *Beginning of the 16th Chapter of St Luke, from the
Earlier of the two Versions ascribed to Wycliffe and
his followers:—about* 1380.*

Forsothe he seide also to his disciplis, Ther was sum
riche man, that hadde a fermour, ether a baily; and this
was defamyd anentis him, as he hadde wastid his goodis.
And he clepide him, and seide to him, What heere I this
thing of thee? yeld resoun of thi ferme, for now thou
schalt not mowe holde thi ferme. Forsoth the fermour
seide with ynne him silf, What schal I do, for my lord

* According to the text published in "The Holy Bible . . . made
from the Latin Vulgate, by John Wycliffe and his followers: Edited
by the Rev. Josiah Forshall and Sir Frederic Madden, K.H." 4 vols.
4to. Oxford, 1850.

takith awey fro me the ferme? I may not delve, I am
aschamyd to begge. I woot what I schal do, that, whanne
I schal be removyd fro the ferme, thei receyve me in to
her housis. And, alle the dettours of the lord clepid to
gidere, he scide to the firste, Hou moche owist thou to
my lord? And he seide to him, An hundrid barelis of
oyle. And he seide to him, Taak thin obligacioun, and
sitte soon, and wryt fyfti. Aftirward he seide to another,
Sothli hou moche owist thou? Which seide, An hundrid
mesuris of whete. And he seide to him, Tak thi lettris,
and wryt foure score. And the lord preiside the fermour
of wickidnesse, for he hadde don prudently; for the sones
of this world ben more prudent in her generacioun than
the sones of light. And I seie to you, make to you
frendes of the richesse of wickidnesse, that, whan ye
shulen fayle, thei receyve you in to everlastynge taber-
naclis.

---

12. *From Trevisa's Translation of Higden's Polychroni-
con, Book I. chap. lix. : as printed by Tyrwhitt in
his edition of Chaucer's Canterbury's Tales, from MS.
Harl.* 1900 :—1385.

This apayringe (*disparaging*) of the birthe tonge is
by cause of tweye thinges : oon is for children in scole,
agenes the usage and maner of alle other naciouns, beth
compelled for to leve her owne langage, and for to con-
strewe her lessouns and her thingis a Frensche, and
haveth siththe that the Normans come first into England.
Also gentil mennes children beth ytaught for to speke
Frensche from the tyme that thei beth rokked in her

K

cradel, and kunneth speke and playe with a childes
brooche.   And uplondish men wol likne hem self to
gentil men, and fondeth with grete bisynesse for to speke
Frensche, for to be the more ytold of.—(TREVISA.) This
maner was myche yused to fore the first moreyn (*mur-
rain, plague*), and is siththe som del ychaungide.   For
John Cornwaile, a maistre of gramer, chaungide the
lore in gramer scole and construction of Frensch into
Englisch, and Richard Pencriche lerned that maner tech-
ing of him, and other men of Pencriche.   So that now, the
yere of our lord a thousand thre hundred foure score and
fyve, of the secunde King Rychard after the Conquest
nyne, in alle the gramer scoles of Englond children leveth
Frensch, and construeth and lerneth an (*in*) Englisch,
and haveth therby ávauntage in oon side and desavauntage in another.   Her avauntage is, that thei lerneth her
gramer in lasse tyme than children were wont to do.
Desavauntage is, that now children of gramer scole kunneth no more Frensch that can her lifte (*knows their left*)
heele.   And that is harm for hem, and thei schul (*an they
shall*) passe the see and travaile in strange londes, and in
many other places also.   Also gentil men haveth now
mych ylefte for to teche her children Frensch.

13. *Beginning of the Reeve's Tale, from Chaucer's Canterbury Tales, after the Text in Wright's Edition,
1847:—about 1390.*

At Trompyngtoun, nat fer [1] fra Cantebrigge,
Ther goth a brook, and over that a brigge,
Upon the whiche brook then stant a melle; [2]
And this is verray sothe that I you telle.
A meller was ther dwellyng many a day;
As eny pecok he was prowd and gay;
Pipen he coude, and fisshe, and nettys beete, [3]
And turne cuppes, wrastle wel, and scheete; [4]
Ay by his belt he bar a long panade, [5]
And [6] of a swerd ful trenchaunt was the blade;
A joly popper [7] bar he in his pouche;
Ther was no man for perel durst him touche;
A Scheffeld thwitel bar he in his hose;
Round was his face, and camois [8] was his nose;
As pyled [9] as an ape was his skulle;
He was a market-beter [10] at the fulle;
Ther durste no wight hand upon him legge, [11]
That he ne swar anon he schuld abegge. [12]

[1] Not far.   [2] Stands a mill.   [3] Mend.   [4] Shoot.
[5] A kind of two-edged knife.   [6] Should apparently be *As*.
[7] Dagger.   [8] Flat.   [9] Peeled (bald).
[10] A swaggerer in the market?   [11] Lay.   [12] Suffer for

14. *From the Persones (Parson's) Tale, in Chaucer's Canterbury Tales, according to Wright's Edition :— about* 1390.

A philosopher upon a tyme, that wolde have bete his disciple for his grete trespas, for which he was gretly amoeved, and brought a yerde (*rod*) to scoure (*score*) the child ; and whan the child saugh the yerde, he sayde to his maister, What thenke ye to do ? I wold bete the, quod the maister, for thi correccioun. Forsothe, quod the child, ye oughte first correcte youresilf, that han lost al your pacience for the gilt of a child. Forsothe, quod the maister al wepyng, thou saist soth; have thou the yerde, my deere sone, and correcte me for myn impacience.

---

15. *From Lydgate's Poem entitled his Testament, according to Halliwell's Text,* 1840 :—*about* 1450.

During the tyme of this sesoun Ver,
I meene the sesoun of my yeerys greene,
Gynnyng fro childhood stretchith [1] up so fer
To the yeerys accountyd ful fifteene,
B' experience, as it was weel seene,
The gerisshe sesoun straunge of condiciouns
Dispoosyd to many unbridlyd passiouns;

Voyd of resoun, yove to wilfulnesse,
Froward to vertu, of thrift gafe litil heede,
Loth to lerne, lovid no besynesse

Sauf pley or merthe, straunge to spelle or reede,
Folwyng al appetites longyng to childheede,
Lihtly tournyng, wylde and seelde sad,
Weepyng for nouhte and anoon afftir glad.

For litil wroth to stryve with my felawe,
As my passiouns did my bridil leede,
Of the yeerde somtyme I stood in awe ;
To be scooryd that was al my dreede ;—
Loth toward scole, lost my tyme indeede,
Lik a young colt that ran withowte brydil,
Made my freendys ther good to spend in ydil.

I hadde in custom to come to scole late,
Nat for to lerne, but for a contenaunce ;[2]
With my felawys reedy to debate,
In jangle and jape[3] was set al my pleasaunce;
Wherof rebuked this was my chevisaunce,[4]
To forge a lesyng[5] and therupon to muse,
Whan I trespasyd mysilven to excuse.

To my bettre did no reverence,
Of my sovereyns gaf no fors at al,[6]
Wex obstynat by inobedience,
Ran into gardyns, applys ther I stal ;
To gadre frutys sparyd hegg nor wal ;
To plukke grapys in othir mennys vynes,
Was moor reedy than for to seyn matynes.

[1] This is the reading in *MS. Harl.* 2255, *fol.* 60.   In *MS. Harl.*
218, *fol.* 66, it is *stretched.*
  [2] Appearance.   [3] Trick, jest.   [4] Contrivance.   [5] Lie.
  [6] This line seems to be corrupted.   Perhaps *sovereyns* should be
sufferance.

16. *Conclusion of Caxton's English Translation of Higden's Polychronicon :—1482.*

And here I make an ende of this lytel werke as nygh as I can fynde after the forme of the werk to fore made by Ranulph monk of Chestre. And where as ther is fawte, I beseche them that shal rede it to correcte it. For yf I coude have founden moo storyes I wold have sette in hit moo; but the substaunce that I can fynde and knowe I have shortly sette hem in this book, to thentente that such thynges as have ben done syth the deth or ende of the sayd boke of Polycronycon shold be had in remembraunce and not putte in oblyvyon ne forgetynge; prayenge all them that shall see this symple werke to pardone me of my symple and rude wrytynge. Ended the second day of Juyll the xxii yere of the regne of Kynge Edward the Fourth, and of the Incarnacion of oure Lord a thousand four honderd foure score and tweyne.

Fynysshed per Caxton.

17. *A Letter written by Sir Thomas More to his Wife after the Burning of his House at Chelsea, from his "Works," by Rastell,* 1557 :—1528.

Maistres Alyce, In my most harty wise I recommend me to you; and, whereas I am enfourmed by my son Heron [*Jerome*] of the losse of our barnes and of our neighbours also, with all the corn that was therein, albeit (saving God's pleasure) it is gret pitie of so much good corne lost, yet, sith it hath liked hym to sende us such a chaunce, we must and are bounden, not only to be content, but also to be glad of his visitacion. He sente us all that we have loste; and, sith he hath by such a chaunce taken it away againe, his pleasure be fulfilled. Let us never grudge ther at, but take it in good worth, and hartely thank him, as well for adversetie as for prosperitie. And peradventure we have more cause to thank him for our losse then for our winning; for his wisdome better seeth what is good for us then we do our selves. Therfore I pray you be of good chere, and take all the howsold with you to church, and there thanke God, both for that he hath given us, and for that he hath taken from us, and for that he hath left us, which, if it please hym, he can encrease when he will. And, if it please hym to leave us yet lesse, at his pleasure be it.

I pray you to make some good ensearche what my poore neighbours have lost, and bid them take no thought therfore; for, and I shold not leave myself a spone, there shal no pore neighbour of mine bere no losse by any chaunce happened in my house. I pray you be, with my children and your household, merry in God. And devise some what with your frendes, what waye wer best to take for provision to be made for corne for our household, and for sede thys yere comming, if ye thinke it good that we kepe the ground stil in our handes. And, whether ye think it good that we so shall do or not, yet I think it were not best sodenlye thus to leave it all up, and to put away our folk of our farme till we have somwhat advised us thereon. How beit, if we have more nowe then ye shall nede, and which can get them other maisters, ye may then discharge us of them. But I would not that any man were sodenly sent away he wote nere wether. . .

18. *Beginning of Tyndal's translation of the* 16*th Chapter of St Luke, from the second edition of his New Testament* (*as reprinted in the* " *English Hexapla,*" 1841) ; *with the Variations, included within brackets, of the passage as given in his Treatise entitled* " *The Parable of the Wicked Mammon :*"—1534 and 1536.

And he sayd also unto his disciples, Ther was a certayne rych [certain riche] man, which [the whiche] had a stewarde [steward] that was acused [y' was accused] unto him that [hym y'] he had wasted his goodes [goods]. And he called him, and sayd unto him, How is it that I heare [hear] thys of the? Give a comptes [accomptes] of thy steward shippe [steward shypp], for thou mayste [maiest] be no longer [my] stewarde. The stewarde [steward] sayd with in [within] him selfe, What shall I

do [shal I doo]? for my master will [wil] take awaye
[away] from me the stewarde shippe [my stewardshypp].
I cannot digge [dygge], and to begge I am a shamed
[ashamed]. I woote [wot] what to do, that when [whan]
I am put out of the stewardshippe [my stewardship],
they may receave [receyve] me into their houses. Then
called he all [al] his master's detters, and sayd [said]
unto the fyrst [firste], How moche [muche] owest thou
unto my master? And he sayd [said], An hondred [an
c.] tonnes of oyle [oile]. And he sayd to [said unto]
him, Take thy bill [byl], and syt donne [sit down] quickly, and wryte fiftie [write *l.*]. Then sayd he to another,
What owest thou? And he sayde [sayd], An hondred
[an c.] quarters of wheate [wheat]. He sayd to him [said
unto hym], Take thy bill [byl] and write foure scoore
[*lxxx.*]. And the lorde [lord] commended the unjust
stewarde [steward], because he had done wysly [don
wisely]. For the chyldren [children] of this worlde
[thys world] are in their kynde wyser [kind wiser] then
the chyldren [children] of lyght [light]. And I saye
[say] also unto you, make you frendes [frindes] of the
wiked Mammon, that, whan ye shall departe [shall have
nede], they may receave [receyve] you into everlastinge
[in everlasting] habitacions.

19. *Beginning of the 16th Chapter of St Luke, from the Version in what is called Cranmer's Bible (as reprinted in the " English Hexapla," 1841):—1539.*

And he sayd also unto his discyples. Ther was a certayn ryche man, whych had a stewarde, and the same was accused unto hym, that he had wasted hys goodes. And he called hym, and sayd unto hym : How is it that I heare this of the ? Geve accomptes of thy stewardshyp : For thou mayste be no longer stewarde. The stewarde sayde wythin hym selfe : what shall I do ? for my Master taketh awaye from me the stewardeshyppe. I can not dygge, and to begge I am ashamed. I wote what to do, that when I am put out of the stewardship, they may receive me into their houses.

So whan he had called all hys masters detters together, he sayd unto the first : how moch owest thou unto my master ? And he sayd : an hondred tonnes of oyle. And he sayd unto hym : take thy byll, and syt doune quyckly and wryte fyftye. Then sayd he to another : how moch owest thou ? And he sayde : an hondred quarters of wheate. He sayd unto hym : Take thy byll, and wryte foure scoore. And the lorde commended the unjust stewarde, because he had done wysly. For the chyldren of thys worlde are in their nacyon, wyser then the chyldren of lyght. And I saye unto you : make you frendes of the unryghteous mammon, that when ye shal have nede, they may receave you into everlastynge habitacyons.

20. *Sonnet by Henry Howard, Earl of Surrey :—*
about 1545.

The soote [1] season, that bud and bloom forth brings,
   With green hath clad the hill and eke the vale ;
The nightingale with feathers new she sings ;
   The turtle to her make [2] hath told her tale ;
Summer is come, for every spray now springs ;
   The hart hath hung his old head on the pale ;
The buck in brake his winter coat he flings ;
   The fishes fleet with new-repaired scale ;
The adder all her slough away she flings ;
   The swift swallow pursueth the flies smale ; [3]
The busy bee her honey now she mings ; [4]
   Winter is worn that was the flowers bale ;
And thus I see among these pleasant things
   Each care decays, and yet my sorrow springs ! *

[1] Sweet.   [2] Mate.   [3] Small.   [4] Mingles

   * The spelling is modernised in this specimen.

(4. Modern English :—A.D. 1550—).

21. *Beginning of the* 16*th Chapter of St Luke, from the Version in the Geneva New Testament* (*as reprinted in the* " *English Hexapla*," 1841) :—1557.

And he sayd also unto his disciples, There was a certain riche man, which had a stewarde, and he was accused unto him, that he wasted his goodes. And he called hym, and said unto him, How is it that I heare this of thee? Geve acountes of thy stewardeshyp : for thou mayst be no longer stewarde. The stewarde sayd within him self, What shal I do, for my master wyl take away from me the stewardshyp? I can not dygge, and to begge I am ashamed. I wot what to do, that when I am put out of the stewardshyp they may receave me into their houses.

Then called he all his masters detters, and sayd unto the fyrst, How muche owest thow unto my master? And he sayd, An hundred mesures of oyle. and he sayed to him, Take thy obligation, and syt downe quickly, and wryte fyfty. Then sayed he to another, How muche owest thou? and he sayd, An hundred mesures of wheat. then he sayd to him, Take thyne obligation, and wryte foure score. And the Lord commended the unjust stewarde, because he had done wysely. Wherfore the chyldren of this worlde are in their kynde wyser then the chyldren of light. And I say unto you, Make you friendes with the riches of iniquitie, that when ye shal departe, they may receave you into everlasting habitations.

22. *Commencement of Sackville's Induction to the Third Part of " The Mirror for Magistrates : "*—1559.

The wrathfull winter, proching [1] on apace,
With blustering blasts had all ybarde the treen,[2]
And old Saturnus, with his frosty face,
With chilling cold had pearst the tender greene;
The mantles rent, wherein enwrapped beene
The gladsom groves that now lay ouerthrowne,
The tapets [3] torne and every blome downe blowne.

The soyle, that erst so seemly was to seene,
Was all despoyled of her beauties hewe;
And soote-fresh flowers, wherewith the sommers
    queene
Had clad the earth, now Boreas blasts downe blewe; ·
And small foules, flocking, in theyr song did rewe
The winters wrath, wherewith ech thing defaste
In woefull wise bewayld the sommer past.

---

[1] Approaching. [2] Bared the trees. [3] Hangings, leaves.

23. *From Ascham's* " *Schoolmaster:* "—*about* 1563.

Quick wits commonly be apt to take, unapt to keep; soon hot, and desirous of this and that; as cold and soon weary [as soon cold and weary?] of the same again; more quick to enter speedily than able to pierce far; even like over-sharp tools, whose edges be very soon turned. Such wits delight themselves in easy and pleasant studies, and never pass far forward in high and hard sciences. And therefore the quickest wits commonly may prove the best poets, but not the wisest orators; ready of tongue to speak boldly, not deep of judgment either for good counsel or wise writing. Also for manners and life, quick wits commonly be in desire newfangled; in purpose unconstant; light to promise any thing; ready to forget every thing, both benefit and injury; and thereby neither fast to friend nor fearful to foe; inquisitive of every trifle; not secret in the greatest affairs; bold with any person; busy in every matter; soothing such as be present; nipping any that is absent; of nature, also, always flattering their betters, envying their equals, despising their inferiors; and, by quickness of wit, very quick and ready to like none so well as themselves.*

* The spelling is modernised in this specimen.

24. *From Sir Philip Sidney's "Apologie for Poetrie:"—
about* 1580.

The Philosopher, therefore, and the Historian are they which would win the gole; the one by precept, the other by example. But both, not having both, do both halte. For the Philosopher, setting downe with thorny argument the bare rule, is so hard of utterance, and so mistie to bee conceived, that one that hath no other guide but him shall wade in him till hee be olde before he shall finde sufficient cause to bee honest: for his knowledge standeth so upon the abstract and generall, that happie is that man who may understande him, and more happie that can applye what hee dooth understand. On the other side, the Historian, wanting the precept, is so tyed, not to what shoulde bee, but to what is, to the particuler truth of things, and not to the generall reason of things, that hys example draweth no necessary consequence, and therefore a lesse fruitful doctrine.

Now dooth the peereless Poet performe both; for, whatsoever the philosopher sayth should be doone, hee giveth a perfect picture of it in some one by whom hee presupposeth it was doone ; so as he coupleth the generall notion with the particuler example. A perfect picture, I say; for he yeeldeth to the powers of the minde an image of that whereof the Philosopher bestoweth but a woordish description, which dooth neyther strike, pierce, nor possesse the sight of the soule so much as that other dooth. For as, in outward things, to a man that had never seene an elephant or a rinoceros, who should tell

him most exquisitely all theyr shapes, cullour, bignesse,
and particular markes, or, of a gorgeous pallace the archi-
tecture, with declaring the full beauties might well make
the hearer able to repeate, as it were, by rote all hee had
heard, yet should never satisfie his inward conceit with
being witnes to it selfe of a truly lively knowledge ; but
the same man, as soone as hee might see those beasts
well painted, or the house wel in modell, should straight-
waies grow, without need of any discription, to a judiciall
comprehending of them ; so no doubt the philosopher,
with his learned definition, bee it of virtue, vices, matters
of publick policie or privat government, replenisheth the
memory with many infallible grounds of wisdom ; which,
notwithstanding, lye darke before the imaginative and
judging powre, if they bee not illuminated or figured
foorth by the speaking picture of Poesie.

---

25. *Beginning of the* 16*th Chapter of St Luke, from the
version in the Rheims New Testament* (*as reprinted
in the* " *English Hexapla* ") :—1582.

And he said also to his Disciples, There was a certaine
riche man that had a bailifè : and he was il reported of
unto him, as he that had wasted his goods. And he
called him, and said to him, What heare I this of thee ?
render account of thy bailiship : for now thou canst no
more be bailife. And the bailife said within him self,
What shal I doe, because my lord taketh away from me
the bailiship ? digge I am not able, to begge I am
ashamed. I know what I wil doe, that when I shal be
removed from the bailiship, they may receive me into

their houses. Therfore calling together every one of his lords detters, he said to the first, How much doest thou owe my lord ? But he saith, An hundred pipes of oile. And he said to him, Take thy bil : and sit downe, quickly write fiftie. After that he said to an other, But thou, how much doest thou owe? Who said, An hundreth quarters of wheat. He said to him, Take thy bil, and write eightie. And the lord praised the bailife of iniquitie, because he had done wisely : for the children of this world, are wiser then the children of light in their generation. And I say to you, Make unto you frendes of the mammon of iniquitie : that when you faile, they may receive you into the eternal tabernacles.

---

26. *The Reply of Belphoebe to Braggadocio, in the Third Canto of the Second Book of Spenser's " Faerie Queene :"—about* 1590.

"Whoso in pompe of prowd estate," quoth she,
"Does swim, and bathes himselfe in courtly blis,
Does waste his daies in dark obscuritee,
And in oblivion ever buried is :
Where ease abownds yt's eath [1] to do amis :
But who his limbs with labours, and his mynd
Behaves [2] with cares, cannot so easy mis.
Abroad in armes, at home in studious kynd,
Who seekes with painfull toile shall Honor soonest fynd

" In woods, in waves, in warres she wonts to dwell,
And wil be found with perill and with paine ;

L

Ne can the man that moulds in ydle cell   *
Unto her happy mansion attaine ;
Before her gate High God did Sweate ordaine
And wakefull Watches ever to abide:
But easy is the way and passage plaine
To Pleasures pallace: it may soone be spide,
And day and night her dores to all stand open wide."

¹ Easy.   ² Employs, occupies.

---

27. *Description of the Irish Mantle, from Spenser's*
" View of the State of Ireland :"—about 1595.

It is a fit house for an out-law, a meet bed for a rebel,
and an apt cloke for a thiefe. First, the out-law, being
for his many crimes and villanyes banished from the
townes and houses of honest men, and wandring in waste
places, far from danger of law, maketh his mantle his
house, and under it covereth himselfe from the wrath of
heaven, from the offence of the earth, and from the sight
of men. When it raineth it is his pent-house ; when it
bloweth it is his tent; when it freezeth it is his tabernacle.
In summer he can wear it loose, in winter he can wrap
it close ; at all times he can use it; never heavy, never
cumbersome. Likewise, for a rebell it is as serviceable.
For in his warre that he maketh (if at least it deserves
the name of warre), when he still flyeth from his foe,
and lurketh in the thicke woods and straite passages,
waiting for advantages, it is his bed, yea and almost his
household stuff. For the wood is his house against all
weathers. and his mantle is his couch to sleep in. Therein

he wrappeth himself round, and coucheth himselfe strongly
against the gnats, which in that country doe more annoy
the naked rebels whilst they keepe the woods, and doe
more sharply wound them, than all their enemies swords
or spears, which can seldome come nigh them. Yea and
oftentimes their mantle serveth them, when they are neere
driven, being wrapped about their left arme, in stead of a
target, for it is hard to cut thorough with a sword; besides, it is light to beare, light to throw away; and, being,
as they commonly are, naked, it is to them all in all.
Lastly, for a theife it is so handsome, as it may seem it
was first invented for him; for under it he may cleanly
convey any fit pillage that commeth handsomly in his
way, and when he goeth abroad in the night in free-boot-
ing it is his best and surest friend; for, lying, as they
often do, two or three nights together abroad to watch
for their booty, with that they can prettily shroud themselves under a bush or a bank side till they may conveniently do their errand; and when all is over he can in his
mantle passe through any town or company, being close
hooded over his head, as he useth, from knowledge of any
to whom he is indangered. . . .

28. *Beginning of the 16th Chapter of St Luke, from the Authorised Version (as given in the " English Hexapla") :—*1611.

And hee said also unto his disciples, There was a' certaine rich man which had a Steward, and the same was accused unto him that he had wasted his goods. And he called him, and said unto him, How is it that I heare this of thee? Give an accompt of thy stewardship: for thou mayest bee no longer Steward. Then the Steward said within himselfe, What shall I doe, for my lord taketh away from mee the Stewardship? I cannot digge, te begge I am ashamed. I am resolved what to doe, that when I am put out of the stewardship, they may receive me into their houses. So hee called every one of his lords detters unto him, and said unto the first, How much owest thou unto my lord? And hee said an hundred measures of oyle. And hee said unto him, Take thy bill, and sit downe quickly, and write fiftie. Then saide hee to another, And how much owest thou? And hee said, An hundred measures of wheat. And hee saide unto him, Take thy bill, and write fourescore. And the lord commended the unjust Steward, because hee had done wisely: for the children of this world are in their generation wiser then the children of light. And I say unto you, Make to your selves friends of the mammon of unrighteousnesse, that when ye faile, they may receive you into everlasting habitations.

JOHN CHILDS AND SON, PRINTERS.